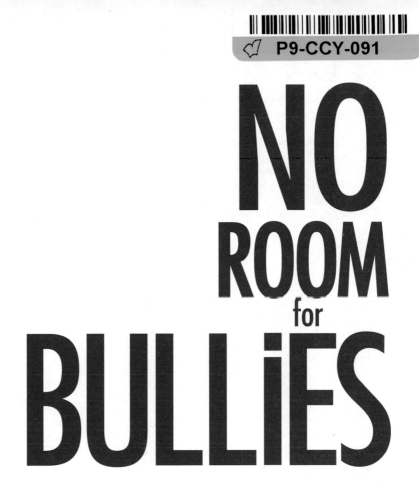

NO ROOM for BULLiES

Also from the Boys Town Press

NO ROOM for BULLiES

From the Classroom to Cyberspace

editors
JOSÉ BOLTON, SR., PH.D., L.P.C., & STAN GRAEVE, M.A.

BOYS TOWN Press SM

Boys Town, Nebraska

NO ROOM for BULLiES

Published by the Boys Town Press
Boys Town, Nebraska 68010

ISBN: 978-1-889322-67-4

The Boys Town Press is the publishing division of Boys Town, a national organization serving children and families.

Publisher's Cataloging in Publication

No room for bullies : from the classroom to cyberspace / editors: José Bolton and Stan Graeve. -- 1st ed. -- Boys Town, NE : Boys Town Press, 2005.

p. ; cm.

Includes bibliographical references and index.
ISBN: 978-1-889322-67-4

1. Bullying. 2. Bullying in schools. 3. Parenting. 4. School environment. I. Bolton, José. II. Graeve, Stan.

BF637.B85 N67 2005
302.3--dc22   0508

10 9 8 7 6 5 4 3

Acknowledgments

This book would not have been possible without the generosity and commitment of many dedicated professionals who work every day to improve the lives of children. The time they spent with us sharing their stories and expertise is greatly appreciated. We would like to say a special "Thank You" to these current and former Boys Town administrators and staff: Tom Dowd, Farrell Artis, Kathleen Brennan, John Fuller, Principal Cathy DeSalvo and staff at Boys Town's Wegner Middle School, Terry Hyland, and Barbara Lonnborg.

Table of Contents

part i

Understanding the Issue

By José Bolton, Sr., Ph.D., L.P.C.,
Stan Graeve, M.A.

Introduction

The teacher in-service began like any other. First, the workshop leaders (from our Boys Town Training Center) introduced themselves. On this day, they greeted three dozen New England middle school teachers who gathered in the school's media room. Their principal had hired our consultants to conduct a one-day workshop on bullying. Having led hundreds of workshops similar to this one, our trainers weren't too surprised that a few participants were somewhat skeptical of the day's agenda. One of the more seasoned teachers was convinced that anything our trainers had to say would be pointless. She was adamant that schools, and especially individual teachers, could do little to stop bullying.

"The apple doesn't fall far from the tree," she said. "Most parents reinforce bullying behavior by giving their kids money to go see movies like *Mean Girls* and they [parents] are bullies themselves."

Our staffers could see nods of agreement from all around the room. It was obvious to them a lot of work had to be done – more work than a one-day in-service could accomplish. Nonetheless, they knew they had to convince these teachers that they can, and must, play a role in changing the social climate of their school. Our trainers have worked with less-than-enthusiastic audiences before, so they were prepared to wow these educators with their reasoned words and researched methods. But before they could launch into the meat of their training, something significant happened. It was a special moment when the pupil became the professor. With a shaking voice and tear-filled eyes, a soft-spoken teacher politely raised her hand and uttered words that resonated through the room more powerfully than anything our trainers could have said or done.

"I was bullied by a group of girls in sixth and seventh grade. I dreaded going to school. I cried myself to sleep at night and wished morning would never come. I never told anyone about what I went through. I didn't even mention it to my parents until last year… and I am 30 years old. To this day, when I see those girls in the store, my stomach gets queasy, and I have to escape. I go to my car shaking. I'm working daily to rebuild my self-esteem. But in a small community like ours, it's hard to avoid those former bullies. If just one teacher can make a difference with one child, it may save that child lifelong pain."

Her candid disclosure crystallized the problem for everyone in the room that day. The skepticism and indifference faded away. And 36 dedicated teachers joined the fight to stop bullying.

Imagine how things might have turned out for this woman if someone – a parent, teacher, counselor, or friend – had noticed her pain. Had noticed how girls in her class constantly mocked her. Had noticed the fear and desperation in her eyes when she was trapped by tormentors on a daily basis. Had noticed her isolation. Had noticed her need for help.

The aftermath of childhood bullying can stay with individuals for a devastatingly long time. It took almost 20 years before this teacher could even talk to her family about her experiences because the shame and embarrassment she felt were so overwhelming and debilitating. Victims may grow older and move on, but many of them never forget. The physical pain of getting punched or shoved may fade, but the emotional pain of being treated as less than human is not so easily erased.

As she said, if just one person had intervened on her behalf, maybe she might not have spent almost the next two decades still feeling like a victim. Sadly, there are adults who still live with the sting of childhood bullying. As much as we would like to turn back the clock and help them change their experiences, we cannot. What we can do, however, is work hard today to make sure no children in our schools and communities are saddled with the shame and indignity that bullying inspires.

Who We Are

This book represents the collaborative effort of many individuals who have distinguished themselves in the fields of parent training, psychology, education, and family development. The authors and contributors include child psychologists who work with young children and adolescents in our Boys Town behavioral health clinics, parent educators who teach parenting skills to moms and dads in our Common Sense Parenting® programs, and education consultants from our Training Center who work with public, private, and parochial school systems throughout our country. Combined, these Boys Town professionals have spent decades "in the trenches." From their first-hand experiences, they show you how to tackle the problem of bullying from every angle:

the school, the home, the neighborhood, the teacher, the administrator, the parent, the bully, the victim, and the bystander. You can read more about our authors on pages 205-207.

The strategies our experts share reflect Boys Town's decades-long history of serving the needs of children and families. Our direct-care programs and services include schools, residential group homes, emergency shelters, foster care, and a national crisis hotline. In all of these services, we work with children and families from every conceivable ethnic, economic, and environmental background. Many of our youth were bullied not only by other children but also by adults, even occasionally by their parents, or were bullies themselves. Given their histories, you might think aggression and bullying are rampant in our schools and programs. They are not. Boys Town's behavioral principles, which are outlined here, succeed because they foster mutual respect, personal responsibility, and connected relationships. These principles can also work in your schools, neighborhoods, and families.

How to Use This Book

We have organized the book into three parts. In Part I, chapters 1 through 3 provide an overview of the problem, including who the players are and how the game of intimidation is played. Chapters 4 and 5 call attention to two issues of growing concern: the use of sexually explicit language and behavior as weapons of degradation, and the proliferation of technology that propels bullying beyond a classroom or neighborhood and into the world of cyberspace. In Chapter 6, we look at why it's important to regularly measure the social climate of schools and programs and how best to do that. Each of these chapters will help parents and educators gain a deeper understanding of childhood bullying. From this increased awareness, we move into specific action plans for administrators, teachers, and parents.

Part II (Chapters 7 through 13) describes the strategies and methods that have proved effective in minimizing bullying behaviors in school and home settings. Chapters 7 and 8 focus on how school officials and program administrators can shape their social environments to reduce bullying behaviors and make every child feel safe and welcomed. Chapter 9 looks at the value of teaching social skills to positively influence the actions of bullies, bystanders, and victims. Chapter 10 speaks directly to parents, offering advice on how to advocate for their children, whether at school or at home. In Chapters 11 and 12, we return to the issues of sexual and cyberbullying. We look at what can be done to stop sexual intimidation and how kids can stay safe and act responsibly when they're using technologies like instant messaging. We conclude the book with Part III that offers additional resources, including a recommended reading list, and other important information for those dealing with the stress, fear, and confusion caused by bullying.

We understand that some chapters will appear to have more relevance or be of greater interest to certain readers. For example, parents who are concerned about online intimidation may choose to skip ahead to the "Safety in Cyberspace" chapter, then turn back to the pages discussing action plans for school officials. Regardless of where your interests lie, we encourage you to read the book in its entirety. No one person or institution can solve this problem alone. The solution requires a consolidated community involvement.

Because bullying occurs where children gather, many of the profiles and examples you will read about involve school-related situations. However, the straightforward approach we emphasize can help you recognize and respond to bullying behavior wherever it happens – on the school bus, in neighborhood parks, even in your own backyard or on the computer at home. You will learn how to improve children's social environments so respect becomes the rule and bullying becomes the exception. Most importantly, you will learn how to help children avoid getting trapped in a cycle of aggression and victimization. In these pages, you'll discover what everyone's role must be and how they must interconnect to create the most supportive and enriching environment for our youth.

chapter 1

By Michael Handwerk, Ph.D.

Defining the Problem

What does bullying mean to you?

How you define bullying probably depends on your experiences. Maybe you were the kid who always had your books knocked out of your hands. To you, bullying involves acts of physical aggression. Maybe you were on the receiving end of snickers and whispers every time you spoke up in class. If so, you may be more sensitive to verbal harassment.

Bullying, as defined by the *American Heritage Dictionary*, means "to treat in an overbearing or intimidating manner." Barbara Coloroso, author of *The Bully, the Bullied, and the Bystander*, describes bullying as always involving three elements: an imbalance of power, an intent to harm, and threats of further aggression. Our definition of bullying is *repeated acts* of aggression or harm (kicking, pushing, excluding, spreading rumors, etc.) by individuals who have *more power* than their victims. By power, we mean advantages in strength, confidence, status, or aggressiveness. However you choose to describe this ubiquitous phenomenon, one thing is certain: Bullying takes many forms, and its consequences damage individuals and learning communities.

As hard as it may be to admit, most of us have behaved like bullies at one time or another, both as children and as adults. This behavior may have involved gossiping, teasing, intimidating, or socially isolating someone. Perhaps we ostracized or excluded a classmate because he or she had unusual hair, wore unfashionable clothes, talked funny, or had some other perceived flaw. Many of us would learn, of course, that acting like a bully was no defense against becoming a victim.

You, no doubt, have at least one memory from your school days when you were the target of a bully's abusive attention. If you can't recall being a victim, surely you remember playing the role of bystander. It was probably just easier to stand and laugh or sit quietly and watch as some other poor soul was picked on, all the while feeling relieved that you were not the one being humiliated.

The bullies that we remember from our youth are a lot like those of today, with one big exception. Today's bullies have new weapons of intimidation at their fingertips. The information superhighway has created avenues for abuse that were not possible when we were growing up. Bullies are now lashing out at their victims using instant messaging on the Internet and text messaging on cell phones. One simple click of a button sends a lie, rumor, or threat to endless numbers of people. We call it "bullying on steroids." It is yet another troubling example of the challenges parents and educators face in the fight to stop bullying.

As we crisscross the country conducting workshops with educators or visiting with parents, we hear a lot about blame. Teachers tell us it's the parents who are at fault. Parents tell us the schools do a lousy job of protecting their children. Children tell us most adults don't want to get involved, and when they do, the situation only worsens. In our experience, there is some truth to what each group says. But playing the blame game will never solve the problem.

The simple truth is this: Bullying can be stopped only if all the stakeholders – from the classroom teacher to the cafeteria cook to the vice principal to the bus driver to the concerned neighbor to the child to the parent – become more vigilant, more skilled, and more proactive. No longer is it good enough to wait until someone is assaulted or a horrifying act of abuse occurs before awareness is raised, accountability is demanded, and action is promised. Reactionary responses are of little consolation or comfort to a victim. And in bullying, all the players – the bully, the bullied, and the bystander – are victims.

How can a bully be a victim? In the short term, research shows that bullies tend to engage in other problem behaviors such as drinking and smoking.[1] Their academic achievement suffers, too. In the long term, without proper intervention, bullies are at greater risk of being incarcerated as adults. In one study, nearly 60 percent of males who were labeled as chronic bullies in junior high (grades 6 through 9) had at least one criminal conviction by the age of 24. And more than 30 percent had multiple convictions![2]

Those who are bullied face dangerous consequences as well. The term "bullycide" was coined to label suicides committed by people because they had been bullied. Depression, anxiety, and alienation can dog victims into adulthood, undermining their relationships and self-confidence, as illustrated by the teacher described in the introduction.

Bystanders have obstacles, too. Fear may be the biggest. Bystanders may hesitate to defend a victim, even a friend, out of fear of what the bully might do to them. They may lack the courage to intervene because stepping up may mean standing alone.

Bystanders may never have been taught how to respond. Sadly, this may partially explain why bystanders often root for the perpetrator and feed the cycle of abuse.

As parents and educators, we certainly can do more to change our children's social environments. We can promote respect, not ridicule. We can ask for involvement, not inaction. We can be partners instead of adversaries, working toward prevention rather than placing blame. That is the message we want to share with you. The perception that bullying is a problem that can't be solved is a false belief. Bullying is a problem that must be solved. Together, we can put an end to the continuous intimidation and harassment that threaten our children's physical and emotional well-being.

In order to address the problem of bullying, we must first dispel many of the myths that surround this issue. Myths are dangerous. They can blind us to the facts. They can lead us toward solutions that are ineffective or impractical. They can focus our attention away from real threats and lull us into a false sense of security. Not surprisingly, there are nearly as many misconceptions about bullying as there are bullies.

To bring a little more clarity to this issue, we've prepared a "Fact or Fiction" Quiz. The following statements are a chance for you to see how well you can separate rumor from reality. You'll find the answers on pages 14-17.

Don't worry if you don't quite manage to score 100 percent. The purpose of the exercise is simply to highlight some truths about who the main players in this drama are, how they act or react to situations, and how their actions can have profound and lasting consequences. There is much more to be said. In the next chapter, you will see profiles of two different types of bullies and types of victims. You will also see why bystanders can be either a child's biggest ally in stopping the cycle of abuse or his or her biggest nemesis.

FACT OR FICTION QUIZ

1. Bullying is a male behavior.   **FACT OR FICTION?**

2. Larger classes and larger schools promote bullying.   **FACT OR FICTION?**

3. Bullies are usually socially isolated.   **FACT OR FICTION?**

4. Bullying is a normal, unpleasant part of growing up.   **FACT OR FICTION?**

5. If told their child is a bully, parents will accept it.   **FACT OR FICTION?**

6. Manipulation, gossip, and exclusion are common bullying tactics girls use.   **FACT OR FICTION?**

7. Bullycide is a term used to describe a suicide caused by bullying.   **FACT OR FICTION?**

8. Most acts of bullying are never reported.   **FACT OR FICTION?**

9. Bystanders who observe bullying violence can be emotionally affected.   **FACT OR FICTION?**

10. Bystanders are always fearful of the bully.   **FACT OR FICTION?**

11. Once a bully, always a bully.   **FACT OR FICTION?**

FACT OR FICTION QUIZ

1. **Bullying is a male behavior...**   **FICTION**
    Bullying defies gender. However, studies show some differences in how bullying is acted out by boys and girls. For example, males are more likely to engage in overt acts, such as punching, kicking, and posturing, while females report using more covert behaviors, such as gossip, rumor, and exclusion. Of course, these behaviors are never gender exclusive.

2. **Larger classes and larger schools promote bullying...**   **FICTION**
    Research suggests that there is no correlation between larger classes or schools and increased incidents of bullying. One Canadian study actually found that students in small schools bullied more. According to the researcher, the findings imply that "Victims of bullying in small schools may be 'repeated victims' because it is more difficult for offenders to select different victims."[3]

3. **Bullies are usually socially isolated...**   **FICTION**
    Research studies show that bullies often enjoy higher social prestige among their classmates. In one large-scale study, bullies indicated a "greater ease of making friends" than did those who were victims or both bullies and victims.[4]

answers

4. **Bullying is a normal, unpleasant part of growing up...**   FICTION

Abusive relationships are not natural, nor should they ever be accepted as normal.

5. **If told their child is a bully, parents will accept it...**   FICTION

Admitting your child is a bully is unlikely given its stigma after high-profile cases of school violence. As parents, we are reluctant to think our children would act in such a way. This underscores the critical need to obtain objective documentation of bullying incidents, especially in schools.

6. **Manipulation, gossip, and exclusion are common bullying tactics girls use...**   FACT

Studies show that girls are more likely than boys to engage in covert behaviors that undermine relationships (gossiping, backstabbing, excluding, etc.).

7. **Bullycide is a term used to describe a suicide caused by bullying...**   FACT

The term "bullycide" was coined by two authors who co-wrote a book by the same name. Suicide is the third-leading cause of death for Americans between the ages of 15 and 24.5 While it's not known how many suicides result from bullying, experts believe it is often a contributing factor for adolescents. Risk factors for suicide include

feelings of hopelessness and social isolation —
two emotions that bullying victims know well.

8. **Most acts of bullying are never reported...** FACT

Research suggests that bullying behaviors often
go unreported for several reasons. Victims feel
ashamed or are reluctant to tell out of fear the
problem will escalate. In our experience, that
fear may be justified. Teachers and parents
who react impulsively often end up compound-
ing the problem as much as adults who choose
to ignore it.

9. **Bystanders who observe bullying violence
can be emotionally affected...** FICTION

Bullying, whether it happens in a school cafeteria or at a neighborhood pool, creates tension
and anxiety in children. It has a detrimental
effect on the entire social climate. At school,
when children do not feel safe, they can't
concentrate on learning. Instead, they focus on
how to avoid being harassed as they walk to
class, ride the bus, or walk home.

10. **Bystanders are always fearful
of the bully...** FICTION

Some bystanders may fear the bully. Others
simply don't know what to do, and still others
worry they'll do the wrong thing if they intervene. Bystanders may exacerbate the situation

answers

by watching, laughing, and generally encouraging the bully's behavior.

11. **Once a bully, always a bully...**   FICTION

No child is a lost cause. With patience, guidance, and instruction, children can be taught how to develop positive relationships with others and satisfy their needs by being assertive rather than aggressive.

answers

1   Olweus, D. (1991). Bully/victim problems among schoolchildren: Basic facts and effects of a school-based intervention program. In D.J. Pepler & K.H. Rubin (Eds.), *The development and treatment of childhood aggression* (pp. 441-448). Mahwah, NJ: Lawrence Erlbaum Assoc.

2   Ibid.

3   Ma, X. (2002). Bullying in middle school: Individual and school characteristics of victims and offenders. *School Effectiveness and School Improvement, 13,* 3-90.

4   Juvonen, J., Graham, S., & Schuster, M. (2003). Bullying among young adolescents: The strong, the weak, and the troubled. *Pediatrics, 112,* 1231-1237.

5   Centers for Disease Control and Prevention. (2003). *National Center for Injury Prevention and Control* [On-line]. Available: http://www.cdc.gov/ncipc/factsheets/suifacts.htm.

By Michael Handwerk, Ph.D.

Profiles of the Key Players

Researchers have identified a number of characteristics and causes that make some children more likely than others to rely on bullying behaviors, and make some children more prone to becoming victims. The reasons vary, from biological to environmental to sociological. We want to share with you some typical traits that have been identified. This is by no means an exhaustive examination. Much research remains to be done, particularly with youth in the United States. However, enough of a consensus exists to provide a general profile of the "typical" bully, victim, and bystander.

The Bully

Contrary to popular belief, bullies are not the friendless, mean loners many people assume them to be. Bullies actually can be quite popular. Many times, they are very connected to school life through athletics, academics, or other extracurricular activities. Bullies generally are strong, confident, and aggressive, much more so than their victims, who, by comparison, tend to be weak, timid, and nonassertive.

Bullies often show aggressive behavior toward adults, including parents and teachers, as well as peers and siblings. They have a need to dominate others, and show little empathy toward their victims. Unfortunately, the behavior of many bullies is partly attributable to inadequately developed empathy and perspective-taking skills. Understanding the feelings of others is difficult for bullies. Usually, they are interested only in satisfying their own immediate wants and desires.

The behavior of children who bully evolves as they mature. Bullying in the early school years (yes, kids can be bullies as early as preschool) tends to involve more verbal teasing and exaggerated body gestures. By middle school, bullies become more physical. Boys commonly will hit, shove, or use intimidating body postures, while girls will start the rumor mill and socially exclude the "undesirables." The middle grades, particularly junior high, are typically when bullying hits its peak. In a study of more than 15,000 American students in grades 6 through 10, nearly 30 percent of youth reported they were involved in some form of bullying, either as the bully, the victim, or both. This same study showed that the frequency of bullying was greatest in grades 6 through 8.[1] Unfortunately, the problem doesn't go away after junior high.

As children grow older, bullying tends to become more covert. In high school, social exclusion and emotional manipulation within relationships are more common. This kind of bullying is very difficult to spot. Nonetheless, its effects can be as damaging to victims as overt acts of physical aggression.

The Henchman

Bullying research has also identified different types of bullies. There is the aggressive, confident type who repeatedly initiates trouble. Then there are those – usually friends of the bully – who are more passive. Individually, they may be reluctant to start harassing anyone on their own. But when their more aggressive friend starts or encourages an attack, they eagerly join in. These more passive bullies are often referred to as "henchmen." Twelve-year-old Sergio is a perfect example.

In class, he is studious and well-behaved. He is helpful when called upon, and not one of his teachers thinks of him as a discipline problem. Because of Sergio's reputation as a polite and friendly student, teachers don't always pay much attention to him when he walks the hallways or sits in the cafeteria. After all, he isn't one of the "problem" kids. When teachers happen to notice Sergio acting up or being aggressive toward another child, they assume it's innocent goofing around. What they don't see is that Sergio's good friend Abram is always nearby when Sergio acts up. Children in the neighborhood and at school know that Abram is a bully. What the teachers don't realize is that the "friendly" teasing they are seeing is actually Sergio continuing the harassment that Abram started.

Henchmen like Sergio serve as an important reminder that bullying incidents are not isolated situations that occur in a vacuum. Often, groups of children are involved. For instance, a female bully can rely on her henchmen to stir up trouble by making them tell another girl (the victim) that her boyfriend was flirting with someone, or that the victim was called an ugly name by a classmate. Bullies use their henchmen as pawns, getting them to do their dirty work. Unfortunately, many adults focus their attention on a single act or child when, in fact, the situation can be more complex, involving larger groups of children in differing roles.

To get at the root causes of bullying, there must be an examination of the entire environment. For example, was the behavior in question age-appropriate teasing or inappropriate intimidation? Who was directly involved, and who was nearby? Was the situation humorous, or did it have an angry, malicious tone? Proper intervention requires understanding. Questions like these can provide the necessary facts to determine if a bullying problem exists, and, if so, how best to respond. We'll take a closer look at how you can identify and respond to bullies and victims in Chapters 6 through 12.

The passive and aggressive nature of children points to an important biological factor: temperament. Young children who are quickly angered or "hotheaded" are more likely to develop into aggressive youth than those who have more relaxed, calm personalities. As a result, the role of parents in fostering appropriate behavior through positive social skills is critical. Children bring to the outside world many of the behaviors they are exposed to in the home. Research tells us that bullies are more likely to come from families where attention and warmth are lacking, where discipline is unpredictable and harsh, and where sarcasm and ridicule are frequent. All of these factors combined with a parent's indifference and detachment are a potent mix for developing aggression in children.

When parents provide little supervision at home, when they tolerate aggressive behavior, and when they behave like bullies themselves, children are much more likely to apply those same behaviors in their relationships. You will find helpful parenting techniques to prevent or correct aggressive behavior in children in Chapters 9 and 10.

The Victim

As we discussed earlier, a bully is someone who repeatedly uses intimidation against individuals of lesser status or power. Therefore, a victim can be defined as someone who is chronically and repeatedly bullied. The most common and troubling characteristic of victims is that they have few, if any, strong friendships to help them through their situations. Not only are victims usually physically weaker, their inability to form close relationships with their peers make them socially vulnerable, too. Victims tend to be sensitive, anxious, and insecure. They lack the social skills that can help deflect bullying, such as knowing how to use humor. When bullied, they often react emotionally – crying, getting angry, withdrawing – which only encourages more abuse. That's how Dominic, a student-athlete from an affluent suburban high school, responded to a bullying incident. His paralysis turned him from a basketball jock into a bully's victim.

In ninth grade, Dominic was the starting guard on his school's freshmen basketball team. He enjoyed playing on a competitive team and winning games. All seemed to be going well for Dominic, and he looked forward to next season. However, when he returned for his sophomore year, Dominic's enthusiasm quickly turned into embarrassment.

It began in the locker room after practice when one of Dominic's teammates, a senior, teased him and suggested that he was gay. At first, Dominic shrugged off the comments and walked away. After the next practice, again in the locker room, the same teammate taunted him again. This time the remarks were as relentless as they were crude. Dominic was embarrassed and hurt. No one had talked to him that way before. Dominic didn't know what to do, so he tried to ignore the other boy. The next day an ugly rumor about Dominic was going around the school. Dominic noticed other kids whispering and snickering when he passed them in the halls. He became increasingly insecure and self-conscious. That afternoon at practice, Dominic's few friends on the team ignored him. Dominic felt isolated and uncomfortable. He started to skip out on team meetings and some practices. For that, he was reprimanded in front of the squad by his coaches. At home, Dominic sulked and stayed alone in his room. His parents assumed it was teen angst. Once gregarious and outgoing, he had become withdrawn and disengaged. He lost interest in basketball and other extracurricular activities. Back at school, the rumors persisted. Dominic decided it would be best if he quit the team and maintained a low profile at school.

Children like Dominic are commonly referred to as "passive" victims, and they represent the vast majority of children who are bullied. Their submissive attitudes and emotional responses play into the power imbalance that exists between bullies and victims. Bullies enjoy seeing the emotional turmoil they cause because it satisfies a need for domination or control. In essence, the victim's reaction is the bully's reward, and a perpetuating cycle of abuse is established.

There are other times, however, when the bully's motives and rewards are much more tangible. Bullies will intimidate victims in order to obtain something of value, such as cash, clothes, candy, CDs, or other items. It's not uncommon for victims to give up a possession as a way to get the bully to back off. Again, victims are manipulated. Worse yet, their reprieve from abuse is almost always temporary.

Victims of bullying lose a lot. Their sense of self-worth, safety, and self-confidence are taken away. They also lose the respect of their peers. Other children, or bystanders, often adopt the attitude that victims "ask for it." Victims are blamed because they won't defend themselves or because they won't conform to what the peer group has defined as normal. That's what happened to

Andre, a very bright junior high student who was bullied because his behavior seemed immature to the rest of his peers.

Andre was a kid who loved math and astronomy almost as much as he loved playing with his toy action figures. At recess, he often played with action figures he brought from home. Other times he read books about the planets and the solar system. Andre's unique interests were not appreciated, nor did they conform to what his junior high classmates considered "normal." They freely and openly shared their opinions. Andre was verbally taunted and ridiculed during recess, where shouts of "nerd," "sissy," and "baby" were hurled at him daily.

Bullies can target anyone, but they particularly enjoy picking on kids who have physical, emotional, or developmental characteristics that set them apart from their peers. In Andre's situation, playing with action figures was odd to his peers because they had long since outgrown such toys and preferred playing team sports, such as touch football and basketball. This is a situation in which a child is bullied for reasons that he or she has some control over. In Chapter 10, you'll learn what Andre did to stop the bullying and how you can empower victims, not blame them.

The Provocateur

As with bullies, not all victims are cut from the same cloth. A small minority of victims, often referred to as "provocateurs," actually encourage – or seem to by others – their own victimization. They may do it as a way of gaining attention or gaining control. How can a victim be in control? For provocateurs, control is gained by occupying another person's time and attention. It doesn't matter to them if the attention they receive is negative just as long as everyone's focusing on them.

The aggression directed at provocateurs often is in response to their own actions. They tend to be restless and easily aroused.

Many suffer from Attention Deficit Disorder (ADD) or Attention Deficit/Hyperactivity Disorder (ADHD). Their annoying behavior provokes hostile reactions from classmates and peers. And, unlike passive victims, provocateurs are not afraid to tease bullies, act aggressively, or perpetuate conflict. The profile of Jalen on page 27 illustrates the dynamic interplay that develops between a provocateur and bully. At times, it seems like role reversal.

Identifying Victims

Victims often have a hard time seeking help. Remember that Dominic, the basketball player, did not talk to his parents or coaches about what happened in the locker room. This is typical of victims who feel ashamed or believe their situation is hopeless. Also, many victims fear retaliation if they report the abuse. Even worse, children sometimes worry that the adults in their lives cannot or will not protect them. When children are unwilling to seek help, it's imperative that adults recognize the subtle and not-so-subtle signs of being bullied. These can include:

- Appearing distressed, depressed, or tearful
- Experiencing a sudden or gradual deterioration in schoolwork
- Being afraid or reluctant to go to school
- Getting teased in nasty ways
- Staying close to teachers or adults rather than peers
- Coming home with unexplained bruises or scratches
- Having torn clothing or damaged books
- Choosing odd routes to go to and from school
- Spending significant time alone
- Needing extra money for no apparent reason

JALEN'S JOURNEY

School wasn't much fun for Jalen. In the fourth grade, he started experiencing social and academic problems. In class, when he was supposed to be listening, he was talking. When he was supposed to be reading, he was fidgeting. He often left his desk in the middle of instruction to sharpen his pencil or go to the wastebasket. On the playground, things were just as chaotic. Jalen constantly interrupted his classmates' conversations or intruded on their games. His sharp tongue belied the fact that he was small in stature. His annoying, sometimes hostile behavior caused many fights. His classmates liked to pick on Jalen just to see how mad he would become.

Not surprisingly, Jalen was pulled out of recess and into detention. This intended punishment actually turned into a reward. Sitting in his classroom instead of going to recess meant Jalen was no longer getting picked on by his peers. His female teacher, whom Jalen thought was cute, would sometimes show him positive attention. Jalen made sure he "missed" recess for much of that year.

In fifth grade, Jalen's problems persisted. He was diagnosed as ADHD. Still small for his age, he now suffered from severe acne. Harassment at school and pressure from his parents overwhelmed him. Jalen started to engage in mild forms of self-mutilation. At school, he sneakily attacked his bullies. He wrote threatening notes, and he stole their school supplies. For his actions, Jalen received numerous office referrals, and his parents were called in for conferences on multiple occasions.

After fifth grade, Jalen's parents enrolled him in private school. The very first week, he was bullied on the playground. Jalen started a fight after being called names like "pizza face" and "shrimp." When the incident was investigated, the boys who bullied Jalen never admitted any wrongdoing. They received office referrals. Jalen was expelled.

Keep in mind that some children will periodically show some of these signs or characteristics and not be victims of bullying. However, the more indicators that are present, the more likely it is that a child may be getting bullied.

The Curious Bystander

Bystanders are easy to see but difficult to describe. Their emotions and motivations differ widely. As discussed earlier, some are passive observers who believe it's not their responsibility to get involved, or they don't want to be known as snitches.

TOMORROW'S PROBLEMS FOR

Many children involved in bullying overcome their situations and go on to lead productive, healthy lives. Yet, research reveals that for some bullies and victims, the trouble doesn't always end when the bullying stops. In fact, it may be just the beginning.

Research suggests that bullies tend to have a more open attitude about using aggression and violence. Dan Olweus, a forerunner in bullying research, describes the typical bully as having an "aggressive personality pattern." If this pattern of antisocial behavior is not dealt with during children's formative years, some bullies appear doomed to lives of desperation. For example,

Olweus found in one of his studies that males who were school bullies were much more likely to be convicted of crimes by the age of 24 than those who were neither bullies nor victims. If that weren't bad enough, that same study showed that nearly 40 percent of the former bullies had at least three criminal convictions.

Other researchers have noted that bullies tend to engage in other unhealthy behaviors such as delinquency and substance abuse, both of which can create a slew of problems later in life. We know that kids who repeatedly skip school are at a greater risk of dropping out. With limited education, chronic

Others are fearful of retaliation. Some go along as a means of self-defense from becoming the next target. There also are bystanders who don't know what to do. You sometimes see them carefully watching to see how adults react, and then they respond accordingly.

Ironically, some victims experience more pain from bystanders than they do from bullies. This happens when victims' so-called friends see them getting attacked yet do nothing. Victims feel betrayed. They feel even more isolated. It becomes harder for them to trust anyone.

TODAY'S BULLIES AND VICTIMS

unemployment is more than just a possibility. Those who struggle with substance abuse undermine their own success as well as that of their families. The cost to society, in terms of social services, can be quite high.

But it's not just bullies whose futures are at risk. For some victims, the freedom of adulthood, which gives them the ability to socialize with whomever they wish in whatever environment they choose, still can't release them from their emotional baggage. In another study by Olweus, former victims who were in their 20s were much more likely to feel depressed and have lower self-esteem than their peers who had not been victimized. Other studies suggest that victims can struggle for years with anxiety, insecurity, and other mental health issues. Tragically, a few of the very troubled never even reach adulthood. Some choose suicide. A very small number violently lash out at their tormentors and others, leaving a trail of death and destruction that tears apart families and communities.

Source: Dan Olweus, "Bully/Victim Problems Among Schoolchildren: Basic Facts and Effects of a School-Based Intervention Program," in *The Development and Treatment of Childhood Aggression* (1991).

Regardless of their motivations, when bystanders watch, laugh, join in, or do nothing, they are supporting and encouraging harassment and intimidation. Kids often tell us that if they're not the ones doing the bullying, they are not part of the problem. That's simply not true. When violence is ignored and overlooked, it starts to become expected and accepted. This is especially true when adults – teachers, coaches, and parents – see bullying yet do and say nothing.

Of course, there are children who are compassionate, secure, and strong enough to intervene. But too often they are the exception, not the rule. That's why parents, educators, and children must work together to create new norms and expectations. Only when the majority stands together and speaks out against the abuse bullies inflict can real change occur.

Children with Multiple Roles

There are children who researchers refer to as "bully-victims." These are the children who bully others but also get victimized by bullies. Research suggests that these children may suffer more than those who are just bullies or just victims. In one study of middle school students, a comparison of bullies, victims, and bully-victims revealed that bully-victims were "by far the most socially ostracized by their peers, most likely to display conduct problems, and least engaged in school."[2]

These are the children who may be at the greatest risk for mental breakdowns. Fed up with the abuse they've endured, they attack others in the same way – or worse – which only compounds their problems. That's why parents and educators must look at bullying situations in a larger framework, to include the circumstances and actions that precede acts of aggression. Was the "bully" also a victim who was retaliating against a tormentor and was the "victim" really a bully who was getting pay-back? With bullying, not every child fits neatly in a specific category. That's why the strategies and action plans described in Part II of the book focus on changing children's behaviors and attitudes, regardless of the role they've played in the past.

---

1 Nansel, T.R., Overpeck, M., Pilla, R.S., Ruan, W.J., Simons-Morton, B., & Scheidt, P. (2001). Bullying behaviors among U.S. youth: Prevalence and association with psychosocial adjustment. *Journal of American Medical Association, 285,* 2094-2100.

2 Juvonen, J., Graham, S., & Schuster, M. (2003). Bullying among young adolescents: The strong, the weak, and the troubled. *Pediatrics, 112,* 1231-1237.

chapter 3

By Michael Handwerk, Ph.D.

The Acts of Bullies

Cheyenne was the envy of every girl in her fifth-grade class. She was pretty, popular, stylish, and smart. Many tried to imitate her in fashion and in action. She was a cult-like figure who had dozens of wannabes all trying to be her best friend. Cheyenne loved all the attention, and she used her popularity to become a master manipulator. She dictated that no girls could wear red shirts or blouses. If they did, she would ignore them and make others do the same. So, no one ever wore red to school. She convinced several boys to eat salt because, according to Cheyenne, "it made them more manly." Every day in the cafeteria, boys sprinkled generous amounts of salt in their hands, then licked it up. They made sure Cheyenne saw or heard about how much they had eaten. Each boy hoped it would prove what a "man" he really was.

● ● ●

MISS AMERICA ON BULLYING

Q. What do you tell your young audiences about your platform, "Preventing Youth Violence and Bullying: Respect Yourself, Protect Yourself," and your own personal struggle with bullying while you were growing up?

A. One of the things I tell them is that, because I am Miss America, they probably think I was homecoming queen and the most popular person at school, but in actuality I did not fit into any of those categories. I tell them that when I was in the ninth grade, I was the victim of severe and pervasive racial and sexual harassment. This included name-calling, teasing, taunting, vandalism of my family's property, and death threats. I was forced to transfer to a different school during the middle of my sophomore year. That was a time in my life when my self-esteem and self-image was assaulted on a daily basis, and really made me question who I was and how I felt about the person I was trying to be. I encourage young people to refuse to let others define them; you have to choose to define yourself on your own terms. I also talk to them about the way in which you rebuild your self-esteem and your sense of optimism: by being involved in community service, retaining the values that are important to you and that you enjoy, and by refusing to allow another person to set limitations upon you based on their stereotypes or misconceptions of what you ought to be.

Excerpt of interview with 2003 Miss America Erika Harold, taken from http://www.pageantrymagazine.com/c03missamerharoldint.html (June 18, 2004)

Cheyenne may seem like a fictional character from an after-school TV special, but she is not. The counselor who shared Cheyenne's story with us remarked that she couldn't believe how much power one innocent-looking girl could have over so many. Cheyenne is an example of what we call an emotional bully. She toyed with her classmates' feelings by dangling friendship and affection in one hand while threatening social exclusion and isolation in the other. The way she played the boys also made her a sexual bully.

The actions of bullies can be divided into two main types: sexual and nonsexual. Behaviors within those types are either covert or overt. When Cheyenne flexed her bullying muscle, she often used covert behaviors. Her subtle intimidation was difficult for adults to detect, but painfully obvious to her victims. According to Cheyenne's counselor, many of the boys who ate salt later admitted that Cheyenne encouraged or dictated their behavior simply by making eye contact with them or by her facial expressions. Across a crowded cafeteria, she would shoot them "a look" of approval or disappointment. Sexual and emotional bullies like Cheyenne can be very smart about how they intimidate their victims. In her best-selling book, *Odd Girl Out*, Rachel Simmons describes the hidden nature of girls' aggression as "typically more psychological and thus invisible to even an observant classroom eye. There is the note that is slipped into a desk; the eyes that catch, narrow, and withdraw; the lunch table that suddenly has no room." As adults, we must be aware that bullying behavior will not always be obvious, public, or out loud.

Chapter 4 offers a revealing look at sexual bullying, from overt abuses like grabbing butts and breasts to the covert acts of language cons and dating violence. Beyond the sexual, bullying can be labeled as physical, verbal, social, and, as Cheyenne brilliantly demonstrated, emotional.

Physical Bullying

Physical aggression is perhaps the most widely recognized form of bullying. Typically, the behavior is overt, involving such actions as hitting, kicking, pushing, shoving, choking, tripping, and punching. These are the kinds of bullying behaviors most people think of when they say, "You know it when you see it." But physical bullying can occur even when there is no contact between bullies and victims. This behavior is often referred to as "posturing" or "posing," and both girls and boys will do it as a way to terrorize and frighten. Posturing can be done in any number of ways. A bully might shake his or her fist, slam doors shut, slam books down on a desk, stare down or glare at someone, toss others' belongings around, or violate others' personal space by towering over them or getting in their face. These are scare tactics bullies use to intimidate. When we catch kids posing or posturing, the reasons they cite most often for their behavior are:

- They simply didn't like someone.

- They wanted revenge on someone who had gotten them into trouble.

- They were jealous of the attention that a girlfriend or boyfriend had given to someone of the opposite sex.

Although their motivations varied, the one common denominator these bullies all shared was a feeling that they couldn't get away with anything more than threatening gestures. They knew a physical confrontation would surely get them in trouble, so they bullied their victims in ways they knew would likely be unseen, ignored, or overlooked by adults. Most times, they were. When you look for signs of bullying, you can't fixate on old definitions or assumptions. Victims may not be getting hit, but the nonverbal messages bullies send their way pack a wallop just the same.

Verbal Bullying

If you remember back to our bullying quiz, you know that boys like to get physical. With girls, it doesn't happen as much. For female bullies, the mouth is as powerful as the fist. As a group, females tend to have better verbal skills at an earlier age than males. This makes them more adept at using words as weapons.

Name-calling, swearing, and using hate speech are a few of the more overt displays of verbal bullying. And just like physical acts, most people assume they know verbal bullying when they hear it. But sometimes what you hear can be deceiving. Verbal bullying is not always the domain of youngsters. For example, as part of a consultation at an urban middle school, our education consultants sat in on a classroom to observe how the teacher and students interacted. In the span of five minutes, the teacher made the following comments:

- "Rachel pay attention."

- "Rachel be quiet."

- "Rachel, you know your art supplies don't belong there. Put them where they belong now."

- "Rachel, do you see how nicely Miguel cleaned up his work station? You need to do the same. Now, Rachel!"

Does Rachel suffer from ADHD? Is she a bad listener? Does she not obey instructions? You might think all of the above, but that would be wrong. Anytime something happened in that classroom, Rachel was singled out and admonished by her teacher – loudly and publicly. This happened despite the fact that other students were not paying attention. Other students were loud. Other students misplaced their art supplies. The teacher's constant nagging and picking at Rachel reverberated outside the classroom. At recess, Rachel's classmates mocked her by mimicking the teacher.

"Rachel, you're stupid!" shouted one girl.

"Rachel, you can't play with us. You don't know how," said a laughing boy.

"Rachel, did you clean your locker yet?" said another.

For whatever reason, the teacher had it in her mind that Rachel was responsible for the classroom's chaos. The teacher's harsh tone and constant badgering had a ripple effect. If the teacher could nag Rachel, then it must be okay for others to do the same. This is a disturbing example of how easy it can be for adults to bully children and not even realize they're doing it. Psychologist

"My childhood was extremely lonely. I was dyslexic and a lot of kids made fun of me. That experience made me tough inside, because you learn to quietly accept ridicule."

– ACTOR TOM CRUISE
As quoted on www.no-bully.com

James Garbarino and therapist Ellen DeLara warn about the dangers of adult intimidation in their book *And Words Can Hurt Forever.* They say, "… adult bullies amplify the effects of peer bullies. They do this by depriving kids of a sense of adults as allies." The result, of course, is that adults, including parents, help create and reinforce a negative and unhealthy environment. Chapter 10 offers advice for moms, dads, and other caregivers on how they can model and teach respect to children.

Other forms of verbal bullying include spreading rumors and gossiping, which are done using spoken words or note-writing. These are sly ways in which bullies try to undermine their victims' reputations and relationships. Maybe they start a whisper campaign that so-and-so cheated on her boyfriend, or maybe they betray someone's confidence by revealing secrets in an attempt to embarrass him or her. Rumors and gossip are also social and emotional forms of bullying. (These are discussed in the next section.) The distinctions between what constitutes verbal, emotional, physical, or social bullying are not always concrete, nor vitally important. However, by labeling the various forms of bullying, you get a better understanding of the problem.

Social and Emotional Bullying

Social bullying occurs when victims lose acceptance or credibility in front of their peers or others because of the actions of a bully. It may involve public humiliation and embarrassment, as when a bully imitates the behavior, voice, or appearance of someone in a demeaning way. Bullies who want to beat up their victims will sometimes make sure that all the kids at school or in the neighborhood know that there will be a fight behind the gym or at an abandoned lot. The fight is a form of physical bullying, but the spectators who gather make the event socially humiliating for the victim, who almost always loses the fight.

A more subtle expression of social bullying involves manipulation. A good example of this is when children are told that they cannot be in a particular social clique unless they dump certain friends or stop (or start) doing certain activities. This is a form of social abuse because the consequence to the victims is exclusion. They are being manipulated by others in order to keep them out of the group. Girls are particularly skilled at engaging in this type of rejection.

Manipulation is also a big weapon in emotional bullying. Repeatedly and intentionally excluding someone from birthday parties or other gatherings is both a social and emotional form of bullying. Treating victims like friends in some situations, but turning on them in others is emotional manipulation. Remember the story of Cheyenne at the beginning of this chapter? She was popular but also vindictive. Kids were afraid not to be her friend. She could dictate the behavior of others because they believed she had the power to make their social lives better or worse. Cheyenne used her social status to manipulate the way girls thought they had to dress, and what some boys thought they had to eat. Regardless of the methods bullies choose to attack, abuse, or exploit their victims, the bottom line is that the behavior is inappropriate and unacceptable.

chapter

By Kathleen McGee, M.A.

Sexual Bullying

"When I say the word ho or bitch, I know there are a lot of people, they take it one way, but when I say them I desexualize the words basically because I'm talking about both sexes. You might be messing around with your boys and call your boy a bitch. And men are ho's all the time."[1]

When rap artist Ludacris was challenged by critics who said his liberal use of "bitch" and "ho" in his lyrics demeaned women, he dismissed their concerns by cleverly redefining the meaning of the words. Apparently, "bitch" and "ho" are not meant to stigmatize and dehumanize females. According to this rapper, they are genderless descriptions meant for friend and foe alike. But, you can see how his meaning might get lost in translation when you consider these lyrics:

Move bitch, get out the way
Get out the way bitch, get out the way
Move bitch, get out the way
Get out the way bitch, get out the way

Who bought these f---- TVs and jewelry bitch,
  tell me that?
No, I ain't bitter, I don't give a f---
But I'ma tell you like this bitch
You better not walk in front of my tour bus

— LUDACRIS IN "MOVE BITCH"

Sexualized and degrading language heard in song, on screen, and in the street is so mainstream, it's almost mundane. Today's adolescents are inundated with so much sexual imagery and lingo that many have become desensitized to the words and the behaviors. They often can't see anything wrong with using words once considered taboo in polite conversation. For example, adolescents often ask us why we make such a big deal about the word "bitch." They don't consider it offensive, so why should we? Our response to them is, "Do you want to be thought of as, or treated like, a dog? You shouldn't."

Young people don't always realize the power and violence in words. When they become desensitized to hearing vulgarities, then repeat them in conversations, their language becomes what they allow. Their behavior begins to parallel their words. As vulgar language and gestures become more pervasive, children and adults become more tolerant of the behavior. Suddenly, what was once impolite, rude, or outright offensive, is now considered normal. This is especially true in regard to children's and teens' perceptions about intimacy. "Banging," "screwing" and "knocking" are a few of the more mild yet common slang terms used to describe sex. But even these words imply aggression and violence. So synonymous are the two in music videos, motion pictures, and popular magazines, adolescents can't help but have a somewhat distorted idea about sex. Popular culture provides our young people with other distorted "norms" as well: sexual intimidation is okay; aggression in dating relationships is typical;

violating personal boundaries is no big deal; showing respect is a sign of weakness; and signs of disrespect show strength.

As responsible adults and parents, it's difficult for us to imagine our kids being confused about what is and is not acceptable and appropriate behavior. And we certainly can't imagine our children getting involved in sexual bullying or harassment. However, a study sponsored by the American Association of University Women and released in 2001 suggests that the disturbing values of pop culture are being put into practice by an astonishing number of youth. The study's survey of more than 2,000 public school students in grades 8 through 11 revealed the following:[2]

- Eight in 10 students experience some form of sexual harassment by peers.

- Six in 10 students experience some form of sexual harassment often or occasionally.

- More than half of the students say they have sexually harassed their peers.

- Students who experience sexual harassment are most likely to react by avoiding the person who bothered them, talking less in class, and not wanting to go to school.

Being Overtly Sexual

What does it mean when kids say they are being sexually harassed? Chapter 2 provided profiles of the typical bully and the tactics he or she uses. Bullying is manipulation and intimidation in relationships. At its most fundamental, bullying is aggression, and sometimes that aggression is expressed in sexual ways. Here are some common behaviors bullies use to sexually and emotionally torment their victims:

- Pulling clothes off (including yanking down pants and shorts), flipping up skirts or dresses, and tugging shirts or snapping bras

- Touching, grabbing, or pinching parts of the body, including the chest, buttocks, and groin

- Forcing physical contact, including kissing, hugging, and other intimate acts

- Flashing private parts and "mooning"

- Writing sexual messages or graffiti in public spaces or on personal property

- Using derogatory language, including bitch, faggot, dyke, ho, and slut

- Showing or leaving behind sexually explicit pictures, images, drawings, notes, and other material

- Making sexually suggestive comments, jokes, and gestures

- Spreading sexual rumors

- Asking intimate questions, such as, "Are you a virgin?" or "How many sex partners have you had?" or "What color are your panties?"

Bullies who use these tactics often defend their behavior the same way Ludacris defends his rap: It's all a simple misunderstanding. When caught or challenged about what they did, you will hear bullies say things such as, "I was just joking with him (or her)" or "I didn't mean it *that* way." Victims, who are already feeling shame and embarrassment, then start to question what really happened. Their self-doubts can include thoughts such as: Maybe I did misinterpret the situation; maybe I am too sensitive; maybe it was just an innocent gesture or joke; maybe I did something to deserve it.

All of this second-guessing is exactly what bullies want their victims (and any bystanders) to think. Bullies can avoid punishment while still manipulating and controlling their victims. As adults, when we hear or see kids saying or doing anything that makes others feel uncomfortable, intimidated, or scared, we need to respond. The target, or others who observe or feel the effects of hostile behavior, get to define whether the actions are sexual intimidation, not the harasser!

More Myths Revealed

Hopefully, the statistics we've highlighted will dispel any misconceptions you have about the extent to which sexualized bullying goes on among our youth. But it's not just the pervasiveness of the problem that should trouble you. There are other myths that adults buy into that keep our children at risk. One is that when boys engage in sexually aggressive behaviors, they are just acting "normal," or their behavior is excused because "boys will be boys." A second myth is that girls don't use sex to intimidate or bully. There are countless victims who beg to differ. If adults dismiss as innocent the sexual aggression of one gender or cannot believe the other gender is even capable of such behavior, how can anyone be surprised that 60 percent of our kids end up being sexually harassed, repeatedly, by their peers? Too many people are missing too many signs.

Ignoring or casually accepting questionable behavior opens the door for kids to engage in more frequent and severe acts of aggression. Take this example that occurred at a suburban high school's prom. A "tradition" had begun two years earlier when a group of senior guys decided they would have more fun if they removed their shirts during the last dance of the evening. They, along with several underclassmen, partially disrobed to the applause and squeals of their classmates. The chaperones observed what was happening but remained silent. The next year, a new group of guys willingly stripped off their shirts for the last dance, although a few had to be goaded by their friends and their dates. Seeing the dance floor turn into a mosh pit of flailing arms and naked torsos offended some. Others in attendance felt uncomfortable watching the bare-chested boys gyrate and rub up against their dance partners, but they, too, said nothing. After all, it just seemed goofy, and it was "tradition."

In spite of the misgivings that many chaperones and parents felt, no one publicly voiced any concerns. The behavior was ignored for three years. No one recognized that maybe this behavior was contributing to a sexually charged environment that went beyond prom night. It wasn't until sexually aggressive behaviors and suggestive comments became all-too-frequent occurrences at the school did anyone begin to recognize that the last dance "tradition" was part of the problem.

Now, you may think that the behavior on the dance floor was innocent and okay. At a different time, in a different place, it might be. But the purpose of this prom was to teach young people how to relate to one another in a social environment. Just as it wouldn't be appropriate for you to attend your employer's holiday party and get drunk, it's not appropriate for these young men to strip on the dance floor. Their actions created a hostile environment for those who felt uncomfortable, and their dress violated the standards that existed for a school-sponsored dance. The nonresponse response by the chaperones had the effect of

INNOCENT TRADITION OR SEXUAL INTIMIDATION?

Perhaps no other subject is colored in more shades of gray than sexual harassment. Very often, a single incident evokes opposing opinions. Deciding if a situation is innocent or indecent, cruel or comical, can be one of the most challenging decisions for educators and parents. When the circumstances surrounding an event are ambiguous or open to multiple interpretations, there is often disagreement. Here is a classic example:

A senior awards banquet at Des Moines (IA) Roosevelt High School had fewer honorees after a parent complained about categories like "Best Butt," "Best Body," "Best Legs," and "Dirty Old Man." The parent called the awards "sexist, inappropriate, and harassing." School administrators appeared to be at odds over whether or not such categories were offensive and should be eliminated. A vice principal was quoted as saying, "I don't see where it borders on sexual harassment. It's just a kind of fun thing that kids do every year. They've been doing this for years." A member of the school board thought differently, saying those categories were "clearly crossing the line and could be considered sexual harassment."

In the end, school officials sided with the parent and excluded the awards. The decision was a disappointment to some students. One said, "I think parents are making too much of a big deal out of it. I think kids are just having a good time with it." Another offered this opinion, "For some of the seniors, that might be the only award they ever get in their high school years. I would feel happy if I got one."

Other awards to be given out included:
- Biggest ego
- Biggest fake-baker (artificial tanner)
- Biggest partier
- Most desirable to be stuck on an elevator with
- Most likely to date a freshman

Source: Dana Boone, "Awards for 'best butt' & 'best legs': Harmless or sexist?" *Des Moines Register* online, April 13, 2005.

creating a social climate ripe for abuse. Adults rationalized their acceptance of the behavior by labeling it a tradition. Prom-goers assumed what they were doing was okay because the chaperones didn't complain. The silence from adults was deafening. In the end, what would seem to be obviously unacceptable was now completely acceptable.

Needless to say, our recommendations for improving the social climate of this high school included putting an end to the prom tradition. To do this, school officials needed to clarify and publish a code of conduct for prom and other formal school functions. The code included consequences for anyone who was in violation of the rules. To ensure that everyone understood the new expectations, a school assembly was held prior to prom where the students were given a copy of the conduct code. A second copy was mailed to each student's home. These changes were part of a larger effort that included training for teachers and support staff to recognize and respond to aggressive behaviors in classrooms, common areas, and throughout the school grounds.

Aggression in Relationships

Not all sexualized bullying is as visually obvious as groping someone or flashing one's privates. One of the most dangerous, yet difficult to recognize, acts of aggression occurs in dating relationships. Studies show that adolescents who bully are more likely to engage in sexual harassment and exhibit dating aggression than those who do not bully.[3] This underscores the dangers that exist when children's aggressive behaviors go unnoticed or unchallenged.

In relationships, bullies will often use language cons (words and phrases) to trick or manipulate their targets into doing things they shouldn't. Language cons can seem very innocent, or they may be terribly graphic. They may make a person feel good, or guilty, or threatened, or trusted. They may be sly, or they may be overt. Most of the time, they are used to persuade a person into keeping a secret. They always are used as a means of control. Common language cons include comments such as these:

- *"Just this once. Trust me."*
- *"You know I wouldn't do anything to hurt you."*
- *"This is normal. This is the way it's supposed to be."*
- *"If you love me, prove it."*

Aside from convincing a target to have sex, the sexual bully may try to talk his or her victim into doing other things that can lead to trouble. These commonly include running away, drinking alcohol or using drugs, stealing, or getting revenge on someone. Regardless of what the desired outcome is, the process is usually the same. The sexual bully will build a false sense of trust, keep the relationship secret, and then manipulate the victim into doing whatever the bully wants. These excerpts of real letters confiscated from students illustrate how a bully can use language to build "trust":

> *"I'll treat you right, and I'm not going to do anything behind your back. You are what I live for. So without you my soul is black and my heart is empty. It might sound like I'm trying to get over on you but I'm not. I mean everything I say. It comes from the heart. I cry almost every night hoping I could be with you. You're the best I ever had."*

> *"We can't let anyone break us apart. If we get into an argument or disagreement we will work it out. People here can't be trusted. Only trust me."*

Individuals who are most susceptible to falling prey to language cons are those who desperately want attention and affection. They also tend to have unhealthy or poorly established boundaries. Ultimately, victims feel powerless and afraid. They're at a loss as to what to do. The best chance victims have to escape and avoid further abuse is to tell someone who can help, like a trusted adult, older sibling, or friend.

While it's ideal to have victims or bystanders come forward on their own to report acts of sexual harassment, the statistics suggest many don't. The good news is that there are many things parents can do to counteract young people's involvement in, exposure to, and use of sexually degrading language and behavior. We'll talk about those strategies in Chapter 11.

[1] "Ludacris Desexualizes Bitch & Ho," viewed at http://rapdirt.com/article344.html, November 1, 2004.

[2] Lipson, J. (Ed.). (2001). *Hostile hallways: Bullying, teasing and sexual harassment in a school.* Washington, D.C.: American Association of University Women Educational Foundation.

[3] McMaster, L.E., Connolly, J., Pepler, D.J., & Craig, W.M. (2002). Peer to peer sexual harassment in early adolescence: A developmental perspective. *Development and Psychopathology, 14,* 91-105.

By Laura Buddenberg

Bullying in Cyberspace

Bullies thrive in permissible environments. These are places where adults are not present (literally and figuratively) and where bystanders do not intervene on behalf of victims. One place where bullies appear to be roaming free is cyberspace. It is a high-tech playground for intimidation. Almost any verbal, social, sexual, or emotional bullying that can be done face to face is being done online, often anonymously. Rumors are spread. Threats are made. Reputations are ruined.

The wave of technology sweeping into our homes and schools offers as many challenges as opportunities. Like anything else, technology is only as good as the individuals who use it. Bullies are taking advantage of the ease and speed of the Internet to humiliate their victims before an audience of thousands. Cyberbullies create Web sites and Web journals (blogs) to post ugly comments and unflattering pictures. They use e-mail to spread rumors and send sexually explicit material. They use instant messaging to "virtually" exclude and embarrass.

Even the ubiquitous cell phone is a tool that is used to text-message threats. The old, protective barriers of time and place (being out of sight and out of mind) that once shielded victims from continuous torment no longer exist. Anyone, anywhere, at any time, can be victimized.

The good news for our kids is that most schools have controls in place that make it unwise for anyone to send harassing messages using a school computer. There is usually some type of paper trail that makes tracking down the culprit(s) much easier. And the consequences can be quite severe. The bad news is that similar safeguards often don't exist outside the school. For that reason, much of this chapter focuses on what parents need to know. However, the intimidation and harassment going on in cyberspace has consequences for educators, too. Online bullying often turns into confrontations at school and vice versa. One day it's a shove in the back, the next day it's an instant message threatening a punch in the mouth. Each act of aggression feeds another. To end the cycle of abuse, parents and teachers must recognize how some students are using the Internet as a tool to intimidate and humiliate.

IM Online

According to the Pew Internet and American Life Project, as many as 17 million children between the ages of 12 and 17 go online.[1] For their parents, it seems the biggest worries are identity theft and adult sexual predators. Few seem to be aware of a much more likely danger lurking on the Web – kids bullying kids.

A popular online service known as instant messaging (IM) is perhaps the most preferred weapon of intimidation for bullies. Instant messaging is basically a real-time version of e-mail that allows users to engage in back-and-forth dialogue instantaneously. Many IM software programs can be downloaded for free from the Internet by anyone. You may have IM on your computer, thanks to your kids or their friends, and not even know it. But you wouldn't be the only parent in the dark. We conducted a workshop on Internet bullying for a group of junior and senior high school students in rural Nebraska. We put the students in one room and their parents in another. When we asked the students how many use IM, 90 percent said they do. But when we asked their parents if their kids use IM, three-fourths did not know or answered "No." Many simply had not heard of instant messaging or how it worked. If you're unfamiliar with IM, here's what you should know.

Most IM programs allow users to create "buddy lists." These are contact lists that contain the screen names of people they want to keep track of, usually friends and family. Generally, when a user launches the IM application on the computer, the buddy list will highlight the screen names of individuals who also are currently online. The user can then select an active name from his or her buddy list, type a brief message, and hit send. The message receiver typically responds instantly, and the two can engage in a real-time "convo" (IM lingo for conversation). Skillful IM users can carry on multiple conversations at one time. For example, Sarah may be messaging Serena about where to go to find prom dresses while, in another dialogue box or window, Sarah's arguing with her boyfriend because he didn't wait for her after school. In addition to one-on-one messaging, most IM programs have chat functions that allow users to invite several people from their buddy lists into a group discussion while excluding others. Think of IM as the ultimate party-line telephone, and your kids are surely dialed in. Even if you don't have a home computer, your kids can gain access to IM at school, the home of a friend or relative, the public library, or an Internet café.

A 2004 *Washington Post* article reported that there were 36 million screen names in use through AOL's free instant-messaging service. Of those, 25 percent belonged to individuals younger than 17.[2] One teenage girl even admitted to us that she uses three different screen names so she can "spy on her friends." As many as 13 million teens use instant messaging.[3] IM is especially attractive to junior high kids who are more social and tech-savvy than their elementary-age counterparts, but still lack the mobility older teens enjoy. For many 11- to 15-year-olds, IM is their social currency. Instant messaging allows them to bring their social lives home. They continue conversations or fights started at school. They gossip. They plan for the weekend. They do homework. They talk about the big game. They goof on each other. They argue. They trash talk. They chat about who likes who. They share their thoughts and their secrets.

IM Myths

Much of what our kids say online is done without the knowledge or supervision of parents. And even if parents know that their kids use instant messaging, most assume it's as innocuous as the telephone. What may be more disturbing than parents' indifference or failure to recognize IM's potential for abuse are the many misguided notions kids have about chatting online. Among the myths, none may be more harmful than these:

All conversations are private.

Hardly. Comments made online are as public as words scrawled on an Interstate billboard. It's there for all to see. When you hit the send key, you no longer control the message. You may have typed, "for your eyes only," but that won't make it so. Messages, or very select portions of them, can be cut, copied, and pasted, then forwarded on to people who were never supposed to see them. E-mails and instant messages can easily be printed out, then passed around. These are the kinds of situations most kids fail to anticipate when they get caught up in the rush of instant messaging. And it's not just that messages can go to anyone, anywhere. Kids can't see the person or persons they're chatting with, so they can never be too certain who's really reading their messages.

A dirty trick bullies like to play using IM is to bait their victims into making comments about someone who the victims don't realize is part of the conversation. That's what happened to 14-year-old Stephanie. She was surfing the Web on a Friday night when she received an IM from her classmate Charlotte. Charlotte was one of the most popular girls in school, and belonged to a social clique that Stephanie wished she could be part of. Charlotte's IM asked Stephanie if she could explain the history assignment from that day. Stephanie was more than eager to reply. She thought this was her chance to be accepted by the in-crowd. After a brief chat about the assignment, Charlotte started asking Stephanie about what she thought of Molly, another classmate of theirs.

Charlotte asked, "Did you see Molly's hair... a blind guy must have styled it!!"

Stephanie laughed to herself and replied, "Yeah... pretty bad."

Charlotte then messaged, "She must get her clothes out of a dump!!"

Stephanie was so excited to be chatting with Charlotte that she didn't really care what was being said. She hastily responded, "Molly's NASTY!!"

That was it. There were no more IMs from Charlotte. She had logged off.

At school on Monday, Stephanie discovered her "private" chat with Charlotte wasn't private at all. Molly and several other girls from school had been at Charlotte's house. They were all sitting around the computer, watching the conversation, and deliberately thinking of ways to get Stephanie to say something bad. Stephanie was crushed. She felt violated. Charlotte, Molly, and the other girls told everyone at school that Stephanie was two-faced. Of course, Stephanie hadn't really meant what she said in her message. But it was too late. Charlotte used Stephanie's own words against her, and reversed the situation by making Stephanie look like the manipulative, untrustworthy one. Stephanie lost her reputation, and she lost friends.

Sharing personal information is okay.

Kids who use IM often like to brag about how many names they have on their buddy lists. For them, the buddy list is a status symbol. The more names they have, even if they don't really know who everyone is, the more "popular" they must be. Kids are swapping and copying screen names from each other as wildly as they once traded Pokémon cards. As a result, they are opening themselves up to contact with people they barely know, or don't know at all. Worse yet, some take their openness too far and make the mistake of sharing their private passwords.

With someone's password, you can log on to a messaging service and assume that person's identity. For cyberbullies, it is the ultimate jackpot. What could be better than saying hateful things or spreading vicious lies under someone else's name? Bullies can mess up personal relationships without detection. Even friends and siblings can abuse passwords. A friend might use it to play a prank, or a brother might use it to get revenge. Regardless of the motive, if someone hijacks an online identity, the results can be truly harmful. Here is a story that one parent shared with us:

Keysha and Kadeem had a typical sibling relationship – they argued and annoyed each other often. One afternoon, they got into a knock-down, drag-out fight. Keysha accused Kadeem of stealing her favorite CD. She tore up his bedroom searching for it. Kadeem denied taking the CD and told her to get lost. He accused her of losing it and said she just wanted someone to blame. Keysha called him a liar and a thief, then stormed out of the house. Kadeem was mad, and he took revenge. He logged onto the family's computer using his sister's password. He then sent instant messages to names on her buddy list. Posing as Keysha, Kadeem bragged about stealing other girls' boyfriends and pleasuring them sexually.

In the days that followed, Keysha was flooded with nasty IMs and e-mails. Everybody on her buddy list and beyond, it seemed, had read her brother's lies. She received dozens of hate messages. She had sexual propositions from people she didn't even know. When unwelcome messages came in, she used the "block" function to stop future messages from those screen names. But the messages kept coming. When someone was blocked, he or she simply created a new screen name, again and again if necessary. Keysha was mortified. Kadeem was embarrassed. He never imagined how quickly or how widely his remarks would circulate. But once the send button is clicked, there's no taking it back. Eventually, Keysha trashed her entire buddy list, opened a new account, and created a new password. This time she kept her password private, not sharing it with her brother or her friends.

Bullies don't live in cyberspace.

When we ask young people if they have ever experienced cyberbullying, most say no. But when we get more specific, asking them if anyone has ever called them names, started rumors about them, or harassed them with unwanted messages, they quickly change their tune. Kids know that bullying is wrong, but they don't always recognize it, especially online.

In cyberspace, you can enjoy anonymity. You can pretend to be someone else. You can spy on others' conversations behind their backs. You can get caught up in the moment. Because you aren't face to face, you lose nonverbal cues. You can't read body language or hear voice inflections. Messages can be intentionally manipulated or unintentionally misunderstood. Either way, feelings can get hurt. The very nature of the medium seems to give kids the "courage" to be more outrageous, more suggestive, more blunt, more crude, or more cruel than they ever would be in person. In fact, 37 percent of kids who go online admit that they have said things they would never say in person.[4]

For young Internet users, emotional boundaries, self-restraint, and common sense seem to go out the window. Here is a real IM conversation that went on between two teenage girls who had never even met in person before:

KATIE: "god it sounds like matt had more fun with you then he ever does with me."

ELIZABETH: "now that isn't true!!!!!!!"

KATIE: "he is gonna cheat… so I will have nothing to live for anymore… so im gonna just plan on killin myself sometime soon. I wish you weren't gonna let him cheat Elizabeth, its not fair to me… but I guess if you want to let him that's fine… ill just start planning on how its gonna end for me… I'm not good enuf 4 matt"

ELIZABETH: "u r good enuf 4 him!"

KATIE: "matt hates me, you hate me, and im going to kill myself and if you send this convo to him in an email like you did the last one… im going to kill myself right now"

Does Elizabeth believe Katie is in emotional pain, or that she's just a drama queen? Is Katie trying to manipulate Elizabeth into not seeing Matt anymore, or is this a cry for help? Is Katie suicidal? Elizabeth can't see Katie, so she doesn't know if she's crying or laughing. Likewise, Katie doesn't know if Elizabeth is showing genuine concern or feigning interest while she chats away in a half-dozen other convos going on at the moment. Who's being real? What's really being said? In cyberspace, there's no way of knowing for sure.

In Chapter 12, you will learn how to create boundaries for children when they use instant messaging, the Internet, and other technologies. You'll also find a sample Internet contract you can use with your kids and advice for helping them use technology safely and responsibly.

---

[1] Pew Internet and American Life Project. (2001). *Teenage Life Online* [On-line]. Available: www.pewinternet.org.

[2] Edwards, E. "Buddy Lists and Mixed Messages," *The Washington Post Online,* http://www.washingtonpost.com/wp-dyn/articles/A64312-2004May3.html

[3] Pew Internet and American Life Project. (2001). *Teenage Life Online* [On-line]. Available: www.pewinternet.org.

[4] Ibid.

chapter

By **Ray Burke, Ph.D.,**
Jo C. Dillon, and Denise Pratt

Assessing the Bullying Climate

Much of our discussion in this chapter deals with information that administrators and teachers can use to measure the safety of children's social environments in structured settings. such as schools. However, this information is also appropriate for parents and caregivers who want to learn how schools and programs in their communities can become more proactive in identifying potential problems, such as bullying.

While some of the information-gathering techniques discussed on the following pages are fine for parents to use, others are not designed for use in the home. For example, we would recommend that parents spend time talking with their children about what goes on at school, observing their behaviors, and listening to their concerns; however, we would not recommend that parents hand their children surveys to fill out at the dining room table. If parents hear or observe something about bullying or harassment that troubles them, they should take those concerns to the school. If administrators are also actively assessing the social climate, a more accurate and complete picture of the situation will develop. The more information that is shared between the home and the school, the more effective the intervention efforts will be. (Parents can learn more about creating a cooperative relationship with their local schools in Chapter 10.)

Sources of Insight

How does a teacher or principal know if bullying problems are affecting children in their classroom or school? Many young people don't talk openly about bullying. Being bullied is never fun, so it's not surprising that victims will be reluctant to relive the experience by sharing painful or embarrassing details with others. And bullies like to attack their victims out of earshot and eyesight of adults. That means it's difficult for adults to know about all the bullying that's taking place in schools. Our experience indicates that even the best-managed schools and programs have to deal with bullying. As a result, fully understanding the breadth and depth of the problem requires seeking information from a variety of sources. Some of the best include:

- Office Referral Data

- Injury Reports/School Nurse Data

- Informal Conversations with Staff, Parents, and Students

- Informal Observations

- Surveys

Office Referral Data

Building administrators can use office referral data to answer some of the who, what, where, when, why, and how often questions related to bullying and harassment incidents. For example, office referral data can answer many of the following questions for school administrators:

- Where do most of the referrals occur? Was the cafeteria, restroom, locker room, hallway, and/or parking lot the biggest problem area?

- What did students do to earn their referrals? Did students vandalize school property by writing on desks or damaging computers? Did they destroy others' possessions?

- What time of day did most students get into trouble? Was it in the morning, during the lunch hour, or at the end of the day?

- Which students are causing most of the problems? Who is in the top 10 for referrals related to physical or verbal aggression directed at other students or staff, and what services might they need to address their problems?

In one school we worked with, office referral data indicated that hallways were relatively calm during morning hours but became chaotic during and after the lunch periods when more students arrived late for class. These tardy students were involved in horseplay that often led to verbal and physical fights. This information allowed school administrators to focus their limited resources on addressing afternoon attendance problems with closer monitoring of transitions from lunch to class and announcements about the expectations for student behavior during those times. Office referral data can be used to identify the people and places that pose a risk and help guide development of effective interventions.

Injury Reports/School Nurse Data

Records of a school nurse are sometimes overlooked as potential sources of information regarding bullying situations. A closer review of why children seek medical attention may reveal patterns that signal a bullying incident. For example, are students being "injured" in unsupervised playground areas or areas of the building where there are fewer adults monitoring the hallway? In one school we visited, students passed through a Z-shaped corridor on their way to physical education class. It was an isolated hallway with little adult supervision where some students were doing handstands and others were trying to balance atop a railing and harass others who were walking through the area. Of course, when any adult entered the corridor, all of the students would scatter like seeds in the wind. Nurse reports might be the only source of information about what goes on in this location because adults were rarely there to refer problem students to the office. The point of using injury reports is to be aware that other possibilities for student injuries may exist and to take a more inquisitive approach by asking questions.

> "In the end, we will remember not the words of our enemies, but the silence of our friends."
> - DR. MARTIN LUTHER KING, JR.

Children who have recurring visits to the nurse could be another indication that a bullying problem exists. For example, is there a student who frequently visits the nurse's office at certain times of the day? Does he or she complain about having a headache or stomach pains during a particular class period? It may be that the child struggles with the subject and wants an excuse to get out of class. Or, perhaps the child doesn't eat breakfast and is hungry long before lunch. Or, the student could be the target of bullying, intimidation, or harassment in the class, and he or she simply wants to avoid pain and embarrassment. Again, summarizing data from injury reports or visits to the nurse is another way of identifying potential problems.

Informal Conversations with Staff, Parents, and Students

Administrators of schools and youth clubs should always try to reach out and be available to their stakeholders, especially on issues of safety. Teachers, support staff, and volunteers who work with children on a regular basis often are a good source of information about problems and what can be done to address safety concerns.

Talk to staff.

Informal conversations can begin with a simple e-mail message or handwritten note from an administrator to staff members. It might say something like, "Our goal is to make this school (or program) as safe as possible. If you are concerned about the safety of a particular child, worried about aggressive behaviors, or feel that areas of our building appear less safe or lack proper supervision, please let me know. I'll be talking with each of you over the next few days and will summarize a variety of safety information for discussion at our next staff meeting."

A note to all staff helps set the expectation that more informal conversations will occur. Assure staff that the goal of these conversations is to identify areas that may be unsafe, not to get staff in trouble. Then, work with staff to develop strategies to help address the problem areas. These informal chats are just another way of obtaining information from those who often have the most experience with the problem.

Talk to parents.

Conversations with parents or caregivers are an often-underused way of learning more about children and their school environment. There are many opportunities to have informal conversations with parents such as at parent-teacher meetings, when parents are dropping off or picking up students, or during a phone call to report on a student's success. Unfortunately, too many parent contacts occur after the student has had a problem. Contacting a parent is much easier and advantageous when things are going well. For example, if a teacher or principal sees a child doing something well, he or she can call the child's home, share positive information about the child, and ask a couple of additional questions about school safety.

If a teacher or administrator makes just one or two calls a day, at the end of two weeks, as many as a dozen parents can be contacted. Sharing positive news with parents and hearing their ideas and suggestions, especially when things are going well, makes conversations much easier and enjoyable for everyone. Informal conversations also help to build relationships between adults. The more comfortable parents become with administrators and staff, the more willing they will be to bring up sensitive issues and share concerns in ways that attack the problem rather than the school or its administration.

Talk to children.

Just as it's a good idea for administrators to seek feedback from as many staff members and parents as possible, it's also important for them to talk with lots of students. Asking questions of students, such as "How are things on the playground?" or "Have you noticed anyone having problems in the locker room?" might reveal the presence or absence of a bullying problem.

Another way to obtain information about bullying or harassment problems is to contact the student council. Most student councils have representatives from each grade, so a nice cross-section of the student body is available at one time. When talking to these students or other similar groups, safety and bullying issues should be introduced in a way that's nonthreatening. In other words, we want students to feel comfortable discussing what's really going on. A school official might begin the conversation like this: "We want our school to be safe for everyone. That's why we do lots of different things to improve safety, like keeping doors locked when you're in class and having fences around play and exercise areas. Another aspect of safety is keeping students safe from each other. We know that sometimes kids can get physically and verbally aggressive, which can be unsafe for others. That's why I want to ask you a few questions. If anyone doesn't feel comfortable answering them, that's okay. You can speak to me privately later. Okay?"

After explaining the reasons for asking about issues of safety, school staff can ask specific questions, such as "Are there areas in the building where some students don't feel safe?" and "Are there things that have happened that we don't know about because no adults were around?"

In a group setting like this, it's important to emphasize with students that what is said in the meeting remains in the meeting; that is, meeting participants should not be sharing with classmates what one or several students discussed in the meeting. Personal questions should be avoided in favor of more collective questions that emphasize how to make the social environment more safe and welcoming for everyone. These same kinds of discussions can go on in youth clubs and sports leagues. Creating small focus groups made up of team captains or club leaders is another way to bring kids to the table to talk about peer relationships and safety issues.

An individual conversation with a staff member, a parent, or a child may not always provide the most complete picture or produce the most reliable information. But when all the stakeholders are given opportunities to share their thoughts – through many different forums – the social climate can reveal itself.

Informal Observations

Observation simply means being attentive to what's happening in the environment. For example, when students walk down the hallway during passing periods:

- Is anyone watching to see who's bumping into others or shouting derogatory comments? In one school we visited, we counted nine students who hit classmates with a fist during a three-minute passing period. No adults stopped the aggressive students.

- Does anyone see the couple making out on the stairwell? (This happened during a lunch period when students were supposed to be in class or the cafeteria. Four staff members walked past the students without telling them to stop or get to lunch or class.)

- Does anyone look to see how many students still wander the halls after the bell sounds, or how long it takes them to get where they're going? (In one middle school, during the first 15 minutes after the tardy bell, we counted an average of 80 students in the hallway. Teachers were in their classrooms beginning their lessons with close to half the students in the hall.)

- Does anyone keep an eye on the student who was sent to the hallway because he was disrupting the class?

(In another middle school, two males were put in the hallway for talking back and arguing with the teacher. During 10 unsupervised minutes, these two students knocked on other classroom doors, made faces to students in the class, and slid down the hall as if they were stealing second base. Finally, a security guard arrived to take the students to the dean's office.)

Building administrators have more than a full schedule. However, scheduling informal observations (along with all the formal teacher observations) is much like having a savings plan. Deposit your resources into your account at the beginning of the month, not at the end of the month when there are little or no resources left over. Likewise, schedule time each day for informal observations during the school day. Collect data during observations (e.g., the number of students in the hallway per minute during class instruction time) that will help you assess whether the situation is improving. These observations, and the subsequent strategies for addressing any observed problems, can keep disruptive and aggressive behavior to a minimum. A number of intervention strategies discussed in the next chapter – including reclaiming "unowned" areas – can bring more structure to the physical environment and safety to the social environment.

Surveys

Surveys are an efficient way of measuring children's social environments, especially in school settings. Surveys can assess how students are feeling, as well as capture the opinions of parents and staff. Kids know better than anyone what goes on in their school relationships and what their peer culture is really like. Surveys can help educators and parents get a general sense of what kids have to deal with in their peer groups. There are many advantages to using surveys:

- Information can be gathered from an entire student population (or a representative sample) at one time, which is less time consuming than having individual conversations with each student.

- Surveys provide a safe and anonymous way for children to share their thoughts without fear of exposure or retaliation.

- Surveys can help students feel more comfortable about sharing information because the fear or anxiety of having to talk to an adult is removed.

- Surveys make it possible to track progress. In an education setting, surveys can be administered in the fall, shortly after kids start their academic year, and again in the spring. An intervention plan usually is implemented based on information gathered in the initial survey. The second survey is helpful in measuring changes in the frequency or severity of bullying incidents.

A good survey should be easy to read and designed to measure how safe children feel. Surveys don't have to be long and complex, although it is important that they are valid instruments (i.e., they are measuring what they are supposed to measure). At the heart of the matter is whether or not kids are and feel safe.

One of the best things about surveys is that they provide anonymity to children who may be too embarrassed, ashamed, or fearful to talk publicly about their experiences. It is this sense of comfort or security that can empower students to be more forthright than they might otherwise be. That's why it's important for those who administer surveys to know how to maintain privacy. If children suspect someone other than trusted adults might be sneaking a peak at their comments, they may not be as honest in their answers. We recommend the following guidelines when administering a bullying survey:

- Provide adequate physical space. If necessary, move desks or tables farther apart so students are comfortable and not seated too closely to one another.

- Provide a separate, blank sheet of paper so children can cover their answers as they complete the survey.

- Remind students that they are not to put their names on the survey, and that they must keep their eyes on their own survey.

- Allow no talking while the survey is being taken. Everyone should remain quiet until the last person has completed his or her survey. After everyone has finished, remind students that their answers are confidential and that they do not have to tell anyone how they responded to any question.

- After they finish, students should turn their surveys face up or face down, whichever way will hide their responses. If the survey is printed on both sides of a single sheet of paper, students can use a blank sheet of paper that staff provide to cover their surveys. Another option is to put a coversheet on the survey. It's a good idea to have the name of the survey and the day's date on the coversheet. This reduces the likelihood that the survey will get mixed up with other surveys, and the date is a reminder of when the survey was administered. That's important when follow-up surveys are given so changes can be tracked over a specific period of time.

- **Students should not collect completed surveys.**
  Adults should administer the surveys and pick them
  up. Or, each child can hand in his or her own survey.
  However it is done, avoid having completed surveys
  passed from one student to another.

Sample Surveys

The surveys at the end of this chapter were designed for
education settings and serve as a guide for the types of questions that are appropriate to ask students. Sometimes, surveys
will not be an appropriate way to gather information, especially
with very young children or in situations where they're impractical. When we work with young children or children who are in
shelters and treatment centers, we sometimes replace written
surveys with a verbal exercise. The first thing we do is define bullying. Describing bullying behaviors is important because many
children, regardless of age, don't associate certain aggressive
behaviors with bullying. (Others want to label everything, even
an isolated comment, as bullying.) With young children, it's especially important to identify bullying behaviors such as shoving,
kicking, calling someone names, taking others' possessions, or
refusing to talk or play with someone.

After providing a definition of bullying, we ask the kids to
put their heads down on the table or desk and close their eyes.
We tell them to raise their right arms in the air and make a fist.
We then ask them questions about their experiences with bullying, and they respond by raising their fingers. For example, we
ask them to hold up one finger if they have ever been bullied by
someone at the school, shelter, or wherever we happen to be. The
next question we ask is whether or not they have ever bullied
anyone. We tell them to answer by putting up two fingers.

This simple and easy exercise identifies bullies and victims. By a show of hands, we can get an idea of how much bullying is going on. At the end of the exercise, we thank the kids for their honesty. We let them know that everyone is affected by bullying, that bullying is a serious issue, and that by working together, we can make sure that it stops occurring in this school or setting.

Three sample surveys, including one each for staff, students, and parents, are on the following pages. Additional survey examples can be found in published research or on the Web, or can be obtained from organizations listed in the "Helpful Resources" section. As you read the questions, notice the kinds of information that survey authors try to elicit. As we mentioned earlier, surveys are one of several ways to assess the social climate. We hope you can use these surveys in conjunction with the other information-gathering techniques we've discussed to broaden your assessment efforts.

From Awareness to Action

These first six chapters have exposed common bullying myths, provided profiles of the key players, and redefined what bullying means, including how it is done. From this heightened awareness and greater understanding of the realities of the problem, we can begin to move toward effective intervention. As this chapter explained, to improve our children's social environment, we must open our eyes to what's really going on. We must encourage and reinforce positive behaviors, and respond quickly when bullying and harassment occur.

In the chapters that follow, we will focus on practical solutions for the school and the home. Chapters 7 and 8 look at creating healthy social environments for kids in structured settings, whether it's a school, social club, or sports league. Chapter 9 examines how social skills instruction can be used by teachers and parents to help bullies, victims, and bystanders. And Chapter 10 is a guide for parents on how to reach out and work with school officials when their children are involved in bullying. Finally, Chapters 11 and 12 will discuss what parents can do to address the specific problems of sexual and cyberbullying.

STUDENT OPINION SURVEY

We would like you to answer a few questions about your school. Read each question and pick the best answer. Please try to answer all questions honestly. There are no right or wrong answers.

Your teachers will **NOT** see your answers to the questions. No one will know what you wrote unless you tell them.

THIS IS NOT A TEST. DO NOT WRITE YOUR NAME ON THIS SURVEY.

Your Grade	Your Ethnicity (select one)	Your Gender
O 4th O 7th O 10th O 5th O 8th O 11th O 6th O 9th O 12th	O African American/Black O Asian or Pacific Islander O Caucasian/White O Hispanic/Mexican/Latino O Multi-Ethnic O Native American/ Alaskan Native O Other	O Male O Female
Today's Month		**Year**
O Jan. O May O Sept. O Feb. O June O Oct. O March O July O Nov. O April O Aug. O Dec.		**School**

The following questions relate to bullying in or around your school or on the way to and from your school. Bullying occurs when someone intentionally verbally or physically hurts someone else repeatedly and over time, especially when that person cannot effectively defend himself or herself.

SECTION A

PLEASE INDICATE HOW MUCH YOU DISAGREE OR AGREE WITH EACH STATEMENT.

	Disagree a Lot	Disagree	Disagree a Little	Agree a Little	Agree	Agree A lot
A1. I feel safe at this school.	O	O	O	O	O	O
A2. I have a good relationship with at least one adult in this school.	O	O	O	O	O	O
A3. Teachers take time during the school day to teach us social skills.	O	O	O	O	O	O

FOR THE FOLLOWING QUESTIONS, <u>DO NOT INCLUDE</u> JOKING OR HORSEPLAY WITH FRIENDS.

HOW MANY TIMES DURING THE <u>LAST MONTH</u> AT SCHOOL HAVE...	Not At All	Once	2 or 3 Times	Every Day
B1. You been bullied by other students?	O	O	O	O
B2. You seen or heard others being bullied?	O	O	O	O
B3. You bullied someone else?	O	O	O	O
B4. Others said they were going to hurt you?	O	O	O	O

HOW MANY TIMES DURING THE <u>LAST WEEK AT SCHOOL HAVE YOU</u>...				
B5. Said something nice to another student?	O	O	O	O
B6. Said you were going to hurt another student?	O	O	O	O

	Yes	No	Unsure
C1. Does bullying occur in your school?	O	O	O

C2. If <u>**YES**</u>, please mark all of the areas where you have been bullied, seen others bullied, or you bullied others.

O Lunchroom

O Classroom

O Bathroom

O Halls

O School Bus

O Locker Room

O Outside, on School Grounds

O Online/Text Messaging

O Other (describe): _____

C3. Please mark all of the kinds of bullying that took place when you were bullied, saw others being bullied, or you bullied others.

      O Call Names

      O Hit, Kick, Punch, Push

      O Write Notes

      O Damage Property

      O Exclude or Leave Out

      O Threaten

      O Steal

      O Instant/Text Messaging

      O E-mail

      O Other (describe): _____

	Yes	No	Unsure
C4. If you have been bullied, did you tell an adult?	O	O	O
C5. Did someone in the school (adult or student) stop or try to stop the bullying incident you observed?	O	O	O

C6. If someone stopped the bullying, was it an/a…

      O Adult?   O Student?

C7. If bullying is a problem at your school, what should students or adults do to help stop bullying?

_____

_____

_____

_____

SECTION D

D1. Are there any areas in your school where you DO NOT feel safe?　　　O　　O　　O

D2. If **YES**, please mark all of the areas where you DO NOT feel safe.

O Lunchroom

O Classroom

O Bathroom

O Halls

O School Bus

O Locker Room

O Outside, on School Grounds

O Other (describe): _____

Thanks for completing this survey!

STAFF OPINION SURVEY

We would like you to answer a few questions about your school. Please be as honest as you can when answering the questions. Your responses will remain anonymous.

Darken the circle that best matches your answer. Please use a pencil or black ink and fill in the circles completely.

DO NOT WRITE YOUR NAME ON THIS SURVEY.

Grade You Teach *(mark all that apply)*	Type of Class You Teach	Employed as
O Pre-K or Kindergarten O 4th O 9th O 1st O 5th O 10th O 2nd O 6th O 11th O 3rd O 7th O 12th O 8th	O General Education O Special Education O Combination O Alternative/Other	O Teacher O Paraprofessional O Other

Today's Month	Total Years Teaching	Gender
O Jan. O May O Sept. O Feb. O June O Oct. O March O July O Nov. O April O Aug. O Dec.	O 0-2 yrs O 11-15 yrs O 3-5 yrs O 16-20 yrs O 6-10 yrs O Over 20 yrs	O Male O Female
		School

PLEASE INDICATE HOW OFTEN THE FOLLOWING OCCUR.

	Hardly ever or Never	Not a lot	Sometimes	A lot	Almost always
1. Staff monitor students before and after school (on school grounds).	O	O	O	O	O
2. Staff are present in the halls during transition times.	O	O	O	O	O
3. There are enough staff monitoring students in the cafeteria during lunch.	O	O	O	O	O
4. Students at our school get along well with each other.	O	O	O	O	O

HOW MANY TIMES DURING THE **LAST WEEK,
IN YOUR CLASS, HAVE STUDENTS**...

	Not at all	Once	2 or 3 times	Every day
5. Said something mean to another student?	O	O	O	O
6. Said something nice to another student?	O	O	O	O
7. Taken something from another student to be mean?	O	O	O	O
8. Hit, shoved, or kicked another student?	O	O	O	O
9. Helped another student with something?	O	O	O	O
10. Said they were going to hurt another student?	O	O	O	O

DURING THE PAST **12 MONTHS**...

	0 times	1 time	2 or 3 times	4 or 5 times	6 or 7 times	8 or 9 times	10 or 11 times	12 + times
11. How many times has someone threatened or injured students **on school property**?	O	O	O	O	O	O	O	O

	Yes	No	Unsure
12. Are there any areas in our school where you feel that students are **NOT** safe?	O	O	O

13. If **YES**, please mark all of the areas where you feel students are **NOT** safe.

O Cafeteria   O School Bus

O Classroom   O Locker Room

O Bathroom   O Outside, on School Grounds

O Halls   O Other (describe): _____

We're concerned about the safety of all the students at our school. The following questions relate to the issue of bullying. Bullying occurs when someone intentionally verbally or physically hurts someone else repeatedly and over time, especially when that person cannot effectively defend himself or herself.

On a scale of 1 to 10, with 10 being very serious, how serious a problem is bullying at our school?

1   2   3   4   5   6   7   8   9   10

On a scale of 1 to 10, with 10 being very frequent, how frequent a problem is bullying at our school?

1   2   3   4   5   6   7   8   9   10

Have you observed bullying behaviors?

O Yes   O No

Have you had a student report bullying behavior to you?

O Yes   O No

If you answered yes on either of the previous two questions, where did the bullying occur?

O Cafeteria   O Locker Room

O Classroom   O Outside, on School Grounds

O Bathroom   O Online/Text Messaging

O Halls   O Other (describe): _____

O School Bus

What did you do about it?

O Wasn't sure what to do

O Told the bully to stop

O Talked to the bully/victim about the incident

O Assigned the bully a consequence

O Reported the behavior to administration

O Reported the behavior to parents

O Other_____

On a scale of 1 to 10, with 10 being very comfortable, how comfortable are you with addressing students' bullying behaviors?

1   2   3   4   5   6   7   8   9   10

Which of the following would help you feel more comfortable when addressing students' bullying behaviors?

O More training on how to intervene

O Clearer definitions or a clearer policy on what constitutes bullying

O More administrative support when consequences are administered

O More help supervising "unowned" areas
  (e.g., hallways, restrooms, playground, cafeteria)

O More parental support

O Other_____

In the past month of school, have you set aside class time to talk about bullying with your students?

O Yes   O No

What else do you think we should do as a school to help decrease bullying incidents in our school?

_____

_____

_____

_____

PARENT OPINION SURVEY

We would like you to answer a few questions regarding your child's school. If you have more than ONE child attending this school, please choose ONE child and base your answers on your experiences with the school for this particular child.

Please be as honest as you can when answering the questions. Your responses will remain anonymous.

DO NOT WRITE YOUR NAME ON THIS SURVEY. Please use a pencil or black ink and fill in the circles completely.

Child's Grade	Have you met your child's principal?	Have you met your child's teachers?
O 4th O 7th O 10th O 5th O 8th O 11th O 6th O 9th O 12th	O Yes O No	O Yes O No

Today's Month	Your relationship to the child?	School
O Jan. O May O Sept. O Feb. O June O Oct. O March O July O Nov. O April O Aug. O Dec.	O Mom O Relative O Dad O Other _____	

SECTION A

FOR THE FOLLOWING QUESTIONS, PLEASE INDICATE HOW MUCH YOU AGREE OR DISAGREE WITH EACH STATEMENT. If it <u>does not apply</u> to you or if you <u>don't know</u> the answer, fill in the circle under <u>DNA/Don't Know</u>.

	DNA/Don't Know	Strongly Disagree	Disagree	Disagree A Little	Agree A Little	Agree	Strongly Agree
1. I feel my child is safe at school.	O	O	O	O	O	O	O
2. There is at least one teacher or adult at school my child can talk to if he/she has a problem.	O	O	O	O	O	O	O

The following questions relate to bullying in or around your school or on the way to and from your school. Bullying occurs when someone intentionally verbally or physically hurts someone else repeatedly and over time, especially when that person cannot effectively defend himself or herself.

	DNA/Don't Know	Strongly Disagree	Disagree	Disagree A Little	Agree A Little	Agree	Strongly Agree
3. My child is being bullied at school.	O	O	O	O	O	O	O
4. My child is bullying others at school.	O	O	O	O	O	O	O
5. My child has told me about witnessing bullies at school.	O	O	O	O	O	O	O
6. My child is learning social skills at school that will help reduce bullying.	O	O	O	O	O	O	O

SECTION B

DURING THE PAST **30 DAYS**...

	0 days	1 day	2 or 3 days	4 or 5 days	6 + days
1. On how many days did your child **NOT** go to school because he/she felt it would be unsafe at school or on the way to or from school?	O	O	O	O	O

DURING THE PAST **12 MONTHS**...

	0 times	1 time	2 or 3 times	4 or 5 times	6 or 7 times	8 or 9 times	10 or 11 times	12 + times
2. How many times has someone threatened or injured your child **on school property?**	O	O	O	O	O	O	O	O
3. How many times was your child in a physical fight on **school property?**	O	O	O	O	O	O	O	O

DURING THE PAST **12 MONTHS**...

	Yes	No
4. Have you talked with your child about bullying at school?	O	O
5. Have you discussed your concerns about bullying with school staff?	O	O
6. If yes, do you feel that staff appropriately follow up on your concerns?	O	O

7. If no, what would you like to see school staff do differently in the future?

_____

_____

_____

_____

part ii

Solving the Problem

By Jo C. Dillon
Michele Hensley

Action Plans
for Administrators

It is 11:15 a.m. and the high school cafeteria fills
to capacity. More than 200 freshmen, sophomores,
juniors, and seniors are ready for food and fun. Along
the cafeteria's north wall, underneath a giant mural
of the school's mascot and the slogan, "Joined as one,
we get the job done!" the school's star athletes sit. Not
far from them are tables occupied by cheerleaders
and the status-conscious. A hodgepodge of students
sits in the middle of the cafeteria. African-American
girls occupy a table across from a group of Hispanic
students. There is a table filled with marching band
members, and a table of National Honor Society
students. On the south side of the cafeteria sits what
one teacher half-jokingly calls, "afterthoughts and
leftovers." These are the lowly freshmen, along with
socially dispossessed upperclassmen. Staff members
eat their lunch in a separate room adjacent to the
student dining area. Every day, students and teach-

ers assume their same positions. The adults separate themselves from the youth. The youth separate themselves by status, race, and privilege.

● ● ●

The social environment at this school drips with irony. In spite of their school motto, "Joined as one...," the actions of students and staff suggest little solidarity. In the cafeteria, racially insensitive comments are made. Food is thrown. Aggressive posturing goes on. An absence of adult supervision enables this hostile behavior, which only deepens the divisions among students and their feelings of alienation. The disrespect shown by youth, and the seeming indifference displayed by staff, is a cancer that spreads through the entire school. Abuse and intimidation inspire fear and resentment that cannot be easily contained. This school is a breeding ground for bullying.

Do you recall the warning in Chapter 2 about how adults often focus on a single bullying incident but ignore many of the circumstances that framed the event? Good administrators avoid that mistake. They, as well as their staff, have an awareness of the small issues that can escalate into serious problems. They see the big picture because they understand that the environment has as much to do with bullying as the bully does. For example, schools with healthy social environments have permeable peer groups. In other words, kids interact in a variety of social groups. The same goes for the staff. The challenge for administrators, regardless of their setting, is how to go about cultivating a sense of community and a culture of respect. Healthy social environments are not born from happenstance. They are the result of effort. It's the administrator's job to lead that effort in both word and action.

As discussed in the previous chapter, administrators should constantly collect data to measure the health of their organization. By collecting and analyzing data, problems can be identified and intervention strategies can be developed. The most effective interventions follow two tracks simultaneously. Track one deals with the physical environment, and the immediate steps that need to be taken to keep kids and staff safe. Track two deals with long-term policies that maintain and reinforce healthy, positive elements of the environment. In both tracks, guidelines, expectations, and consequences must be communicated to all the players – bullies, bystanders, victims, staff, and parents – so they understand their responsibilities in maintaining a positive environment. The danger occurs when administrators neglect one or

TEACHERS AND PARENTS HAVE THEIR SAY

- 55% of teachers believe that school districts who back down from assertive parents cause discipline problems.

- 85% of teachers and 73% of parents believe the school experience for most students suffers at the expense of a few chronic offenders.

- 52% of teachers believe behavior problems result from "teachers who are soft on discipline because they can't count on parents or schools to support them.'"

- 46% of teachers and 33% of parents strongly support giving principals a lot more authority to handle discipline issues as they see fit.

From Teaching Interrupted: Do Discipline Policies in Today's Public Schools Foster the Common Good? *survey by Public Agenda, (2004)* both tracks. Actions taken without policies can be arbitrary and biased. Policies with no actions can be manipulated and ignored.

Immediate Steps

Every administrator faces challenges that are unique to his or her organization. The severity of a bullying problem will vary. The kinds of behavior will be dissimilar. The locations where most bullying incidents occur will be different. We understand that interventions work best if they are tailored to an organization's specific issues. However, when it comes to taking immediate steps to improve safety, some actions are universal:

1. Claim "unowned" areas.

2. Train staff members and expect them to be vigilant.

3. Encourage parental involvement.

Claim "Unowned" Areas

Unowned areas, or "hot spots," are where kids feel particularly threatened by bullies. All hot spots have one common characteristic: adult supervision is nonexistent or completely ineffective. Typical bullying hot spots include restrooms, locker rooms, hallways, parking lots, buses, and playgrounds. For an administrator, improving the quality and amount of supervision in these unowned areas is the only way to reclaim them. Gaining control may be as simple as placing an adult where none has stood before. Or it may involve common sense strategies coupled with a little ingenuity. That's how one principal reclaimed a notorious hot spot inside her small town junior high.

The unowned area of the junior high was the boys' restroom on the second floor. Girls walking in the hallway often were grabbed and shoved through the restroom door, then jeered as they ran back out. Groups of guys would often go in, be loud and boisterous, and spend their time goofing around. Directly across the hall from the chaos sat a female teacher in her classroom. The teacher knew when boys were behaving badly. She could hear their crude remarks, as well as the girls' shrieks. Unfortunately, she couldn't always intervene. She would monitor the hallway during passing periods to see who was doing what to whom. But behind the boys' restroom door, there was little she could do. For legal reasons, she didn't want to push open the door, walk inside, and tell the boys to knock it off and get out. She feared accusations of sexual harassment. Men whose classrooms were near the girls' restrooms had similar fears.

In this instance, dealing with the bullying problem meant dealing with gender issues. The principal decided to reposition her entire staff. She made sure there was at least one male staff member near each of the boys' restrooms and locker rooms. Likewise, she had female staffers close to all of the girls' facilities. The simple act of physically moving staff produced several positive outcomes. Staff members stopped using gender as an excuse for inaction. Kids could no longer deflect attention away from their bad behavior with the threat of claiming sexual harassment or impropriety by a teacher. And most importantly, bullying incidents declined because there was much tighter supervision.

Administrators must be as resourceful in their approach to bullying prevention as bullies are in targeting their victims. Bullies are always looking for opportunities to attack. When they see supervision wane, they pounce. Taking ownership of unsupervised areas minimizes threats and provides the first line of defense against bullies by taking away the places where they operate. In some cases, kids may identify hot spots that fall outside the authority or control of an administrator. Regardless, it's still important to know where those locations are, and to make staff, parents, and others in the community aware, too.

Train Staff Members and Expect Them to Be Vigilant

One of our most frustrating experiences as consultants is when people acknowledge that bullying is a problem but then are reluctant to be part of the solution. This is especially true when it comes to supervision, which when done right, can be a powerful deterrent to bullying. People like to pay lip service to the importance of proper supervision, just as long as they don't have to be the ones supervising. The most common excuses we hear include:

- "Watching a restroom is not my responsibility."
- "I get paid to teach, not to baby-sit."
- "I'm too busy to stand out in the hallway."
- "Kids need time to themselves, especially at lunch. We shouldn't hover over them in the cafeteria."

As an administrator, you will hear lots of excuses for why something can't be done. But your job is to point out the benefits of why it **must** be done. Staff members may have to be reminded that good supervision can stop the little behaviors that often lead to big blow-ups. The fewer discipline problems and disruptions staff have to deal with, the more time they have to do the things they enjoy. If the goal is to have a safer, more effective learning environment, the attitudes that allowed bullying to become a problem in the first place have to change.

What we've discovered is that some staff members are not confident in their abilities to monitor kids. Their excuses actually mask self-doubt. As an administrator, you can make supervision

AN ADMINISTRATOR'S CHECKLIST

1. Inform all staff about the dangers of bullying and its effects on children and learning.

2. Create and publicize an anti-bullying policy that defines bullying for students, staff, and parents.

3. Administer bullying surveys at least twice a year, and use that information to formulate action plans and measure success.

4. Devise anonymous ways for youth and others to report bullying incidents.

5. Have trained staff, as well as yourself, monitor and supervise unowned areas.

6. Ask teachers to explicitly explain procedures to students and teach skills that will help bullies, victims, and bystanders.

7. Encourage staff to have regular Class Meetings where students can talk about bullying, do role-play scenarios, and formulate solutions.

8. Ask teachers, counselors, and behavior interventionists to keep track of overt and covert acts of bullying.

9. Follow up with bullying victims so they realize you care, and that they are in a supportive environment.

10. Invite parents, board members, and auxiliary personnel to in-service training workshops on bullying.

11. Maintain parental involvement with regularly scheduled parent meetings.

12. Involve parents, students, and staff in long-term implementation plans designed to foster a healthy, nurturing school environment.

and monitoring less daunting and confusing for staff. Here are some ways to do that.

- **Set up a supervision schedule.** For example, in school settings, staff should be assigned to monitor specific hallways or restrooms during every passing period. If there are four classrooms along one hallway, the instructors should know what passing periods they are responsible for, as well as who they can call on if they need a replacement. All staff should be responsible for checking hot spots when they have free time. This may mean stepping out into the parking lot or keeping an eye on a custodian's room or other secluded area. As an administrator, you also need to make sure everyone is following through on the responsibilities that they have been given.

- **Assign more people to supervise.** Some situations may require one or two staff members, but a crowded playground or cafeteria usually needs several adults so the burden of supervision is shared and kids actually see that people are paying attention to their behavior. Parent volunteers are an excellent resource if staffing is an issue. As an administrator, you also need to be a visible presence to students and staff.

- **Use staff strategically according to their abilities.** Seasoned staffers with lots of experience may be better in hot spots than the newly hired. For example, first-year teachers may not yet have a rapport with kids, or they may be overwhelmed in certain situations, like a crowded cafeteria. Veterans, on the other hand, might garner greater respect. They certainly should have better skills at picking up on potential problems. However, experience can't be the sole criteria. Personality should be a consideration, too. Some staff won't mind getting in the mix with kids while others may be more reluctant. Know the strengths of your staff and use them to your advantage. Those who have excellent supervision skills should be assigned to hot spots.

- **Explain the problem.** Chapters 2 and 3 profiled who the players are and the behaviors that each typically demonstrates. To provide effective supervision, staff need to have the facts, including who the bullies are, what behaviors to look for, and where bullying situations are likely to occur. Data collection allows you to understand the specifics of the problem, but if that information isn't shared with anyone, it's useless.

- **Teach and model supervision skills.** Anyone who supervises youth needs to have vigilant eyes and open ears. On playgrounds, for example, an observant supervisor will pay close attention to children who start grouping together in a particular area. Good supervisors also know how to resolve conflicts, offer effective praise, and use appropriate teaching techniques. Chapter 9 discusses several teaching methods that anyone can use to help bullies, victims, and bystanders.

Encouraging Parental Involvement

Any successful response to bullying has to involve parents or caregivers. Unfortunately, parents often are ignored until there is a big problem. When administrators, staff, and parents are not familiar with one another, problem resolution tends to be awkward and much more difficult. Of course, parents sometimes don't make themselves accessible. They may choose not to respond to outreach efforts because they're too busy or simply indifferent. Overcoming a family's lack of interest can be difficult, but certainly not impossible. The more options families have to be involved, the more likely they are to get involved. As an administrator, you can help your staff reach out to families. Here are a few proactive strategies to consider:

- **Encourage the use of technology to improve communication.** Voice mail, e-mail, and other forms of messaging can complement phone calls or in-person meetings. These mediums can make reaching busy parents easier.

- **Use incentives to get families to come regularly to your school or program.** Something as simple as a pizza dinner or a series of short evening workshops on topics of interest, such as Internet safety, prepping for college, or money matters, might entice parents to visit. Involving their children in these programs can be an effective motivator as well. You may want to have bullying-related materials available for parents to take home.

- **When families do visit, make them feel comfortable.** If language barriers exist, have an interpreter available. Try to understand and respect parents' values, and praise any of the positive things their children have done.

- **Use school-home notes, newsletters, and Web sites.** Newsletters that go home regularly are advantageous because they can inform parents about everything from upcoming events to new policies or codes of conduct that affect their children. Web sites serve the same function, although it's better if the content is not duplicated. Parents should find benefits to reading both. Be cognizant of the fact that many families may not be wired to the Web. Communication efforts should transcend socio-economical, geographical, and cultural barriers.

Parental involvement and input are vital to the success of any program-wide response to bullying. In addition to reaching out to parents, administrators have to be open to their feedback. Parents should be encouraged to come forward if they think their child is being bullied or even if they think their child is prone to being a bully. Kids who witness bullying may divulge that information at home. If parents hear about incidents from their children, they should be urged to bring it to a staff member's attention. As an administrator, you should have a variety of communication channels open and available for staff, parents, and kids to use. Comment boxes, e-mail accounts, or hotlines all encourage feedback and can offer a degree of anonymity if necessary.

Anti-Bullying Policies

Reclaiming unowned areas, improving supervision, and involving parents are key components to any bullying intervention program. However, the individual steps are more effective if they are part of a larger, coordinated plan. A formal anti-bullying policy can provide organizations with valuable direction and protection.

Policies should evolve out of input from staff, parents, youth, and administrators. Included in the policy should be a definition of what bullying is, based on recommendations and suggestions from all of the interested parties. Each organization may define bullying a little differently, but whatever definition is used should be clear and policies should state how the organization will respond when bullying occurs. An ideal policy has at least four other characteristics:

1. Positive behaviors are publicly reinforced.
2. Data collection and reporting mechanisms are emphasized.

BULLYING PREVENTION IDEAS FOR ADMINISTRATORS

1. Be aware of critical data identifying likely places for students to be bullied. Know the frequency and types of incidents that occur. Share data with staff and set goals.

2. Assign staff specific supervision responsibilities. Use them strategically according to their gender, personality, and behavior-management skill levels.

3. Be SPECIFIC with staff members about your expectations for supervising and monitoring students, especially in unowned areas. Staff must know where they are supposed to be and what they need to be doing.

4. Monitor the quality of staff supervision daily and provide positive as well as constructive feedback.

5. Set the example for your staff. Be visible in unowned areas, assist with supervision, and model the behaviors you expect from them.

6. Offer training and support to ALL staff, from bus drivers to cafeteria cooks, to help them prevent bullying situations or intervene when situations develop.

7. Be consistent and focus on improving the social climate every day, not just one special week or month.

3. Consequences are explained.
4. The policy is publicized.

Reinforce Positive Behavior Publicly

More than describing the behaviors that won't be tolerated, anti-bullying policies should define the kind of culture an organization hopes to inspire. At one school we worked with, its policy included a respect pledge that students recited every day following the Pledge of Allegiance. Good policies reaffirm values of respect and tolerance. They include a central guiding principle, such as, "Every child has a right to participate fully in our school (or program), to be treated with respect, and to feel welcomed. Any words or actions intended to segregate, degrade, persecute, or humiliate a member of our community is hurtful to us all and will not be tolerated."

Some anti-bullying policies focus heavily on the negative; in other words, what is not allowed. Everyone understands that when rules are broken, punishment usually follows. Reacting to the negative comes naturally. Recognizing the positive seems to require more effort. But rewarding the good things kids do, even if it's acknowledging the absence of a negative, can be just as or more powerful in shaping their behavior as punishment is. One way to encourage positive behavior is to honor those who exemplify the very ideals that your organization wants to promote. Giving generous praise for acts of kindness and celebrating the good deeds of youth are important if you hope to encourage similar behavior in the future. When kids see their peers being honored or rewarded, they too may want to be showered with similar attention. Here are a few ways to publicly acknowledge young people who have made a positive impact on an organization's social environment:

- **Designate a leader or student of the month.** Honor someone who exemplified positive values, such as fairness or caring, and reward him or her with a plaque, prize, or special privilege.

- **Send notes home or call parents.** Some older adolescents may find being named leader or student of the month more of a humiliation than an honor. However, most young people appreciate praise, and don't mind having their parents hear about what good people they are.

- **Hold a group assembly.** Celebrate once a month with a special gathering and acknowledge groups or individuals who made a positive impact with their peers. Describe what they did and why their actions deserve recognition. Reward them with special t-shirts, caps, or gifts that symbolize their efforts.

- **Have special drawings.** In situations where there is a large number of youth, such as schools, the odds of being named student of the month or getting singled out for special recognition may be small. To help get every child more involved and to give each an equal chance at a reward, try handing out good citizenship tickets, cards, or coupons. Teachers, coaches, administrators, and support staff can hand out these cards to anyone they catch making a positive contribution to the social environment. The kids then write their names on the cards. At the end of each week or month, collect the cards from the youth and put them in a drawing for a special prize or recognition.

Emphasize Data Collection and Reporting

Chapter 6 explained the benefits of using surveys to gauge the social climate of a school or program. When youth complete them anonymously, surveys reveal the where, when, and how often of bullying. By surveying a variety of stakeholders, including staff and parents, you can identify whether perceptions of the problem differ between the various groups. All of the information must be sorted through and evaluated to determine which issues are urgent and how best to address them. With regard to a policy, noting that some form of data collection will be done is important. It establishes an awareness and expectation with stakeholders, diminishing any surprise or distrust they might feel when they're asked for information. In addition, good policies are revised and amended over time. Static policies can fail when circumstances change. Continuous data collection provides the foundation on which improvements to a policy can be based.

Of course, surveys represent only one method of information gathering. Other options include public forums, focus groups, and interviews. One popular method for soliciting information directly from young people is a "comment box." A comment box is sort of like a suggestion box; it allows kids to anonymously drop in notes that describe incidents they've experienced or witnessed. Comment boxes not only provide administrators with valuable feedback, but also offer a safe alternative way for kids to report problems. How to report bullying must also be included in any policy. As an administrator, you have to cultivate the ability of staff, parents, and kids to come forward and share information. You can use your policy to highlight the options available to them, whether it's using a comment box, calling a bully hotline, sending an e-mail to a special account, or talking to a trusted counselor or staff member. The more feedback opportunities people have, the more you are likely to hear.

When you are told about a bullying incident, you need to follow up by gathering as much information as possible. We strongly recommend that you talk to the alleged victim and bully individually, not together. A victim who is intimidated or fearful may downplay or deny that anything happened when the abuser is looking right at him or her. It's also not a good idea because the bully will assume the victim "squealed" and he or she may retaliate or use someone else to get back at the victim.

Explain Consequences

A strong anti-bullying policy makes it very clear that there will be consequences for anyone who violates the rules. However, the policy should not mandate that specific consequences must be applied to specific infractions. There are too many policies written so rigidly that mitigating circumstances become marginalized, if not completely ignored. This is especially true of policies that are based on zero tolerance or the "three strikes and you're out" rule. Sure, that philosophy is easy to understand and makes for a great headline. But too often it becomes an excuse not to spend any time or energy looking into the realities of what actually happened. There usually are some extenuating circumstances that make situations look better or worse than they first appear. It may be an easy decision to expel a child after he gets involved in a fight for the third time, but if you don't bother to investigate whether it was self-defense, or that he had no other options, it may not be the right decision. Ideally, there should be a menu of consequences. Applying those consequences, however, should be based on three criteria:

- The frequency of the behavior
- The intensity of the behavior
- The duration of the behavior

By using the facts of a specific incident and taking into account past history, punishments are much more likely to be sane, fair, and balanced.

When sanctions are used, they should not be delivered in a hostile or physical manner. A calm demeanor and nonjudgmental remarks help to keep the discussion respectful. Additional factors to consider when developing possible consequences include age and environment. For example, in school settings, students may lose a privilege like recess or be suspended from a sports team. In other settings, losing a leadership role or being sent to time-out may be more appropriate. In extreme cases, the law will dictate what happens. Regardless of the consequence, apologies to the victims and some form of restitution should be included.

Make the Policy Overt

A good policy must exist "out loud." If it's filed away, only to be alluded to occasionally or when a crisis occurs, it does more harm than good. A policy has to come to life in the attitudes and actions of individuals. In order for that to happen, its very existence must be publicized and its goals must be understood. When it comes to awareness and comprehension, administrators have a variety of tools at their disposal.

Awareness can be raised by posting the policy in public spaces, such as entryways, dining areas, hallways, classrooms, auditoriums, gymnasiums, and Web sites. If space is limited or if the policy gets lost amid other visual distractions, turn the policy into a campaign. Use eye-popping posters or simple slogans ("Be a Friend" or "Respect Others") to capture the essence and purpose of your anti-bullying initiative. Campaigns offer opportunities for young people to get involved. They should have had input in creating the policy, and they should have a role in promoting it to their friends and family. Kids know better than anyone how to grab the attention of their peers. Best of all, they become more invested in its success. When this involvement occurs, the policy won't be seen strictly as arbitrary rules imposed or dictated by adults. Instead, it becomes a community-wide crusade to promote values such as respect and tolerance.

Another way to raise awareness and make the policy more tangible is to publish it in the form of a handout. Give a copy to every child when he or she registers for school or the program. Hand them to parents during registration and at parent nights, or mail them to their homes. Seize on every opportunity to remind your stakeholders that you value a supportive, inclusive environment.

Awareness, of course, is just the beginning. People have to know what the policy looks like in practical terms. How does it direct decisions? How does it affect interactions? What behaviors are rewarded? What behaviors bring unwanted consequences? What role does the individual play in turning an abstract concept like respect into a concrete, observable act?

One of the best ways to demonstrate the goals and expectations of a policy is through role-playing. Let kids create a skit around a bullying incident, and let them act out all of the roles – bully, victim, bystander, parent, and teacher – during an assembly or parent night. Create different versions of the skit, too. One should have the players doing the wrong things: The bully gets away with his or her behavior. The victim reacts emotionally to the bullying and doesn't seek help. The bystanders look on, laugh, or gang up on the victim. The parents act like bullies in the home or ignore the warning signs that their child is being bullied. The teacher allows disrespectful, aggressive behavior to go on in the classroom. In this scenario, the overall environment feeds a cycle of fear and broken relationships. Follow that version with a skit showing all of the players trying to do the right thing: The victim deflects a bully's abuse with humor or asserts himself or herself in a forceful yet respectful manner. The bystanders intervene by telling the bully to stop, or they invite the socially isolated person to join their group. Staff immediately respond to problem behaviors, and they praise the positive things that kids do. The bully apologizes to the victim. The parents teach their children how to be assertive and follow the Golden Rule.

Use the school play or skit as a metaphor for your policy. By acting out the various perspectives surrounding the issue, expectations are clarified. Everyone sees his or her role and understands how to create a positive, inclusive environment. That's important for the kids and their parents. By making youth active participants, you help to engage their parents. We know that bullying hits its peak in junior high. That is also the same time that many parents become less involved with their children's schools. Parents don't attend "Back to School" nights or other related functions as regularly as when their kids were in the early grades. To reach these parents, you have to give them a reason to show up. Coming to school to hear an educator talk about policy probably won't interest most of them, but seeing their children perform on a stage certainly will.

For older adolescents or teens, performing a skit in front of the student body, staff, and parents may not be too appealing. In high schools, however, there are always "Honors Nights" or award banquets that recognize a sports team, the band, or other school-sponsored clubs. These events have a built-in audience of staff, parents, and youth. Use these gatherings to spread the anti-bullying message. During the program, you can insert a brief 10- or 15-minute talk or video about what is being done to improve the social environment for kids, or recognize individuals who have taken a leadership role in the fight against bullying. Whenever you have a chance to speak in front of any group at school or in the community, drive home the message that bullying is a serious threat to the well-being of youth, and it cannot be tolerated in the community.

The Administrator as Role Model

Administrators have to be agents of change. They cannot delegate all of the responsibilities to improving the social climate to their staff. One of the biggest complaints we hear from teachers is how their principals expect them to solve bullying problems. Principals expect the teachers to go to training workshops and read the latest books on the subject. But the principals, for whatever reasons, don't bother to participate. That leaves many staff members questioning whether or not the boss is serious about making a real difference. These same principals are not walking the hallways with kids or helping to monitor hot spots. They don't use their position to communicate to stakeholders that bullying is unacceptable and will be dealt with. They don't ask staff members if they're having problems with any particular students, and they don't bother to talk to kids, parents, or staff about how safe they feel their school is. If administrators want to make fostering an environment of inclusiveness and respect a priority, they need to get visibly involved and set the appropriate tone for the entire organization.

Strong administrators will communicate the culture they expect to see through their words and actions. They will participate in training programs. They will help staff with supervision. They will seek feedback from staff as well as from students and parents. They will have conversations with stakeholders and answer questions. They will listen when someone tells them what's working and what isn't. They will ask staff if there's a kid whom they're concerned about. They will understand that social issues affect academic issues. They will make safety and a non-bullying environment a priority not only for others, but for themselves.

By Jo C. Dillon
Michele Hensley

Action Plans for Teachers

Sitting on a wooden, four-legged stool in front of his eighth-grade history class, Mr. Johnson decided to quiz his students over the Civil Rights Movement, a topic they had studied for the past week. He told the class to shout out answers after he asked questions aloud. At first, few students spoke up, but the more questions Mr. Johnson asked, the more competitive the students became. Soon, answers were coming from every corner of the room. The more they tried to be the first to answer correctly, the more aggressive the students became, eventually shouting over one another. Half-way through the exercise, there were still a handful of kids who had yet to participate. Mr. Johnson wanted to hear from them, so he asked those five students a question and told everyone else to remain silent. Andrew, who was sitting in the back of the room, was the first to respond to Mr. Johnson's challenge. "I think the answer is Jackson, Mississippi," he said. Before Mr. Johnson could respond, Aaron, who sat on the other side of the room, muttered out loud, "Get a clue. Everybody knows it's Selma, Alabama, you idiot." The class erupted in laughter. Mr. Johnson, who was still seated, looked at Aaron and with a smile on his face, said, "Tell me you didn't just say that." His words hung in the air for a few moments. Then Mr. Johnson turned back to his notes and proceeded to ask another question about civil rights.

• • •

What went on in Mr. Johnson's classroom occurs more often than any of us would like to believe. Blatant acts of aggression happen in front of "responsible" adults, who then act as if they have mysteriously gone blind, deaf, and mute. Mr. Johnson's response was certainly mild, but the message he sent to his students was anything but meek: Disparaging remarks that embarrass classmates are funny and perfectly appropriate.

Mr. Johnson's reaction is what we call the "head-buried-in-sand" approach to bullying problems. The thinking here is that if you ignore or downplay an incident, it will eventually fade away. As a means of intervention, it's a terrible strategy. As a means of prevention, it's even worse. Ideally, Mr. Johnson would have reacted to Aaron's words much more vigorously. He would have stopped the exercise, redirected the class to review their textbooks, gotten up, walked over to Aaron's desk, knelt down to his eye level, talked to him about why his comments were hurtful, and then given him a consequence. Aaron would have lost a privilege and would have been instructed to apologize privately to Andrew. Of course, none of that happened. In many environments where bullying gets out of control, it's precisely because adults act as if they just don't care. Or worse, they only pretend to care.

On the opposite end of the reaction spectrum are teachers, coaches, parents, and others who prefer to fight fire with fire. They yell. They use aggressive body language. They may even get physical. They bully the bully. Their over-the-top responses are done for show or out of sheer anger or exasperation. In the end, their outbursts may make them feel better, but they offer nothing of value to bullies, victims, or bystanders.

So what is a reasonable response? What do you as an educator do to prevent bullying, and what do you do when it happens? How do you react to bad behavior so that it becomes less likely to be repeated, and how do you acknowledge good behavior, such as acts of kindness? Our discussion up to now has focused on the role adults play in shaping elements within the larger environment to discourage bullies. This chapter and the next examine ways to influence the behavior of the individual.

ACCORDING TO TEACHERS

- 52% of America's teachers report their school has an armed police officer stationed on school grounds.

- 77% of teachers admit their teaching would be a lot more effective if they didn't have to spend so much time dealing with disruptive students.

- 34% of teachers have seriously considered quitting because of student discipline and behavior.

- 54% of teachers believe emphasizing classroom management skills in teacher education programs would go a long way toward improving student discipline and behavior.

From Teaching Interrupted: Do Discipline Policies in Today's Public Schools Foster the Common Good? *survey by Public Agenda,* (2004)

Proactive Intervention

We believe one of the reasons that educators such as Mr. Johnson and other adults respond poorly to bullies and their victims is because they never give any thought to how they should react until **after** something happens. As a result, they have to rely on their instincts. In some instances, instincts are good and positive outcomes result. More often than not, however, gut reactions to emotionally charged bullying situations produce extreme responses. Rather than waiting until problems arise and having your emotions dictate your actions, a better option is to use a plan that brings structure to your classrooms or programs and guides your interventions.

For structure to exist, rules must be made, procedures must be followed, consequences must be administered, and social skills must be taught so that children replace their old negative behaviors with new positive ones. This is how a healthy social climate can be created. Without these things, bullies have a free pass to do as they please. Bullying thrives in environments where there is no structure. Whether the setting is a school, an adventure camp, or a family home, kids need to know what they should do and when they should do it. This is especially important when adults are trying to prevent and/or address bullying behavior. The best way to deal with bullying is to have a plan that manages children's behaviors by establishing routines and expectations. To do that, you need to have rules, procedures, social skills instruction, and consequences for good and bad behavior. We begin with a discussion about rules and procedures. In the next chapter, we follow up with how to teach social skills and use effective consequences.

Creating and Enforcing Rules

When we talk about bullying rules, we are not referring to anti-bullying policies, which were discussed in Chapter 7.

Remember: A policy represents a school's or organization's broad vision, and its success depends largely on the skills of administrators. By contrast, rules govern a specific group or activity within an organization, be it a ninth-grade algebra class or a varsity volleyball team. Establishing and enforcing rules is the primary responsibility of teachers, counselors, support staff, and parents who work directly with youth.

Rules are the first layer in a proactive strategy to affect bullying at the individual level. They help to create predictable, stable environments that are much more conducive to healthy, positive interactions. Most schools and classrooms have general rules about behavior, but few have rules specific to bullying. Ideally, rules are simple and declarative. They cannot, nor should they try to, address every conceivable problem that might arise. A laundry list of rules is hard for kids to remember, and even harder for them to follow. Instead, the most effective rules describe general expectations for behavior. Here are a few examples:

- We will respect others physically and emotionally; we will keep hands, feet, and objects to ourselves.

- We will include everyone in our group activities.

- We will help others if they are being bullied.

The Airport Rule

One bullying rule that's proven popular with teachers and kids is the "Airport Rule." Even the most infrequent air travelers know how sensitive airport personnel are to threatening statements or emotional outbursts, even if they are said or done in jest. Aggressive or outrageous behavior by a traveler brings a swarm of security personnel, and the traveler is detained. The same principle can be applied to environments where young people gather: All threatening or negative comments and behaviors are taken seriously, and if a youth is caught engaging in those acts, he or she will be detained. The Airport Rule is a metaphor for how acts of aggression will not be tolerated in any form. And as a rule, it's easy for kids of any age to understand. Here are two examples of how you can define the Airport Rule for youth:

> "If you say hurtful words or make negative comments to others, you will be detained."

> "If you engage in hurtful behaviors or make threatening gestures toward others, you will be detained."

The Airport Rule is useful because it establishes clear expectations and offers a sense of safety. This is especially important to children who might be too afraid to participate or speak up out of fear of being laughed at or mocked. Rules like this can make apprehensive children more willing to engage in activities because they know it's unlikely anyone will try to embarrass them.

Importance of Student Input

Another important characteristic of bullying rules is that they reflect the realities of a given situation. A teacher once came up to us and said very emphatically that rules don't work. She knew this because she had written five rules for her students, posted them prominently in her classroom, and then watched as students ignored **her rules** year after year. When we visited her classroom and talked further, we discovered that **her rules** had never changed in four and a half years! She never gave any consideration to the fact that each academic year ushered in a completely different group of students. Each class had its own collective personality and skill sets. The year she wrote **her rules,** acts of physical aggression were a big problem. Naturally, those behaviors influenced the rules she developed. As time passed, verbal taunting became the big problem; however, no one would have guessed that from reading **her rules.**

Rules designed to prevent bullying have to reflect the behaviors that a teacher, coach, or counselor expects to see from youth; they can be adjusted later according to what really goes on. It might be necessary to have rules that deal with physical contact between kids. Other rules may have to focus on how kids treat each other emotionally. For example, a teacher, before the start of the school year, has to make assumptions about the kinds of bullying that might go on. Those assumptions can be based on experience or feedback from other staff. During the first week of class, the teacher should introduce students to the classroom rules on bullying and other class expectations. After a month of getting to know the kids and observing their behavior, new rules may need to be added or existing rules may have to change. The key is adapting to circumstances and seeking input from the students.

The teacher who complained that her rules were ineffective made no effort to change anything for more than four years. She also didn't seek any feedback from students to find out how the rules could be applied to their daily activities. Most unfortunately, she never bothered to discuss the rules in any depth with her pupils, nor did she practice how to follow the rules. They were just words on paper. There was no praise when rules were followed, nor any consistent consequences given when rules were broken. With no action came zero benefit. Effective classroom rules or codes of conduct involve teaching, in addition to seeking input from and being a reflection of those who are directly affected by the rules – students, team members, or other youth.

Class Meetings

A creative and empowering approach to involving kids in the rule-making process is the Class Meeting. (A more appropriate term may be team or group meeting, depending on your environment.) Class Meetings serve several purposes. They are a great way to develop interest and maintain awareness about bullying, teach social skills, share positive experiences – including praising youth who have worked on improving their relationship skills – and problem-solve issues. (Chapter 10 outlines two creative methods – SODAS and POP – that help children improve their decision-making skills.) Class Meetings can also be used to role-play bullying scenarios, build relationships among group members, and discuss rules, procedures, and consequences. There are three phases to successfully implementing a Class Meeting:

PHASE 1 – An adult (teacher, counselor, coach, or parent) acts as the moderator and models how to lead the Class Meeting.

The basic structure of the meeting, from how often it's held to how long it lasts to where everyone should sit, is discussed. Kids should be active participants in this discussion. Ideally, Class Meetings occur once a week and last anywhere from 10 to 20 minutes, depending on the age of the youth involved. Sitting in a circle or half-circle helps facilitate open communication. Rules governing the conduct of youth during meetings should be discussed. Again, ask kids for their suggestions. A rule might state that only one person can speak at a time or that participants can make only positive comments. You may also want to teach youth how to disagree appropriately. In this phase, the goal is to explain the format and skills necessary to have a productive meeting. Every meeting should also have someone designated to record the topics or issues discussed.

PHASE 2 – Agenda items are developed and discussed.

Youth take the lead in discussing bullying issues. Limit agendas to two or three topics or activities. For example, the first agenda item might be to talk about the definition of bullying. That could be followed by a brainstorming session to identify potential consequences for bullies and bystanders. The final agenda item could be setting goals for the upcoming week. As more meetings are held, discussions can turn into activities where kids role-play scenarios in which they practice positive social skills or act out how to intervene in a bullying situation.

PHASE 3 – Youth are empowered to be moderators and leaders of the meetings.

After showing youth how meetings run and teaching the skills necessary to run them, adults step aside and let the kids take over. (An adult presence is still needed in case conversations get off topic or the moderator loses control.) The benefits of having youth-run and managed meetings are three-fold: 1) Group cohesion is established; 2) Self-government skills are practiced; and 3) Problem-solving and critical-thinking skills are developed.

A Class (or group) Meeting brings everyone together at a designated time to share their ideas and perspectives about bullying, bullying-related rules, and other classroom or group problems. The forum itself emphasizes to kids the seriousness of the issue, gets them actively involved, and holds them accountable for their actions. The rules and behavioral expectations that evolve out of Class Meetings are the first step in influencing the peer culture in a positive way.

While rules help to set standards for behavior, they do not always provide youth with enough behavioral information. In other words, how do rules translate into action? For example, we see the words "Golden Rule" posted in many classrooms. Teachers remind us all the time that they tell kids in the elementary and middle grades to follow the Golden Rule. But what does it mean to treat others as you wish to be treated, especially to a child with a who-gives-a-damn attitude? No one is telling him or her how to show respect. No one is explaining how we are supposed to be "kind" to each other. Rules don't always provide that kind of specificity. Procedures and skills do.

Developing Procedures

Rules help to bring order to an environment, and they describe the behaviors kids should engage in. Procedures, on the other hand, are directions on how to successfully accomplish a task or demonstrate a skill. For adults who want to manage the interactions among youth, procedures can provide the control that's necessary to avert bullying situations. Procedures diminish chaos. The less chaos there is, the fewer opportunities bullies have to lash out. In one classroom we visited, there was a bullying hot spot by the pencil sharpener. The sharpener was on the back wall, far away from the instructor, which made it a popular hangout. Instead of sharpening their pencils right away, boys and girls would elbow each other, stab each other with pencils, and get rowdy. Sometimes the shoving and name-calling would continue as they returned to their desks. To minimize these disruptions, the teacher moved the sharpener to the front of the room so it wasn't so hidden, and she implemented a procedure for using it. First, anyone who wanted to use the pencil sharpener had to ask permission from the teacher. Only one person at a time could be at the sharpener, and each person could take only one pencil.

Procedures are particularly beneficial during times of transition. By this we mean times when kids are on the move, such as going from one class to another, walking to a cafeteria, heading to an assembly, or going to the restroom. Whenever groups of kids are on the move, the potential for problems is amplified. Bullies can shout an insult or give a quick shove, yet avoid detection amid all the commotion. Here are two examples of how procedures can bring order to situations where disorder is common:

Using the Restroom
Three kids at a time may go to the restroom.
There is a three-minute time limit.
Keep hands, feet, and objects to yourself.

Going to the Cafeteria
Walk and talk quietly.
Sit at an assigned table.
Eat food only from your own tray or plate.
Refrain from negative comments or conversations.

Obviously, procedures should fit the age of the youth involved. In our examples, procedures for going to and from a restroom or cafeteria may seem childish or extreme to older adolescents. In fact, many teachers in junior high and high school tell us that they're uncomfortable having formal procedures for teenagers because they believe that teens shouldn't be treated like little children. But, in the same breath, they complain about bullies who have turned the cafeteria or restroom into an attack zone. If the ultimate goal is to reduce the frequency of bullying incidents, then adults must find ways to manage kids' behaviors.

In high schools, a big issue is how kids behave between class periods. When the bell rings, a flood of adolescent humanity spills into the hallways. With so many students in motion and staff few and far between, bullies can get away with a lot. The bedlam during passing periods often results from two very

BULLYING PREVENTION IDEAS FOR TEACHERS

1. Design seating patterns that are easy to supervise, and position your desk to maximize your ability to see the entire room.

2. Remember to occasionally look around and interact with other youth when you are working with one or more students privately.

3. Wrap-up classroom discussions a few minutes before the period ends so you can supervise hallways and interact with students as they transition to other rooms.

4. Look in the restrooms briefly (according to your gender) or call in from the outside and encourage students to hurry up and get to class.

different scenarios that play out in classrooms. Some teachers consistently teach up to and after the bell sounds. The result has kids scrambling to collect their materials and making a mad dash to the door. Meanwhile, the teachers, who should be standing watch in the hallways, are still in their rooms tying up loose ends. The other extreme is when teachers allow kids to huddle around an exit in anticipation of the bell. In the huddle, henchmen and bystanders act as shields for bullies who whisper threats or make intimidating gestures. Once everyone moves into the hallway, it's game on and anything goes.

When large groups of kids move from one area to another, procedures should be in place to manage the ensuing chaos. In schools, that means teachers should try to wrap up their remarks and prepare students for dismissal a minute or two before the class period ends. Teachers should position themselves by the exits and remind students about simple procedures, such as walking – not running – out of class, and avoiding horseplay or roughhousing. As students file out, teachers need to keep one eye on their class and the other on the hallway. Procedures also are an effective way to control the number of kids who enter hallways, cafeterias, gyms, or other spaces at any one time. For example, dismissing kids in intervals based on age, gender, seating position, or other criteria can minimize chaos by thinning out the crowd, and making supervision and monitoring much easier.

The real value of procedures is the specificity and guidance they provide for an individual's behavior. Procedures establish and encourage positive and productive actions, which undermine the ability of bullies to create chaos or fear. Together, rules and procedures are useful in shaping behavior. But their long-term influence is severely limited if young people are never taught how to follow them. That's why social skills instruction has to be included in any plan to help bullies, victims, and bystanders. For young people to handle difficult situations and interact with one another on a personal level, they need social skills.

In the next chapter, you will see how certain social skills can address the behaviors that bullies, victims, and bystanders struggle with. Nine specific skills are highlighted and each is broken down into its behavioral steps. Explanations of why these social skills are important and how you can introduce and reinforce them to youth are provided.

chapter 9

By Jo C. Dillon

The Role of Social Skills

Social skills are sets of behaviors that give individuals the ability to interact with one another in ways that are socially acceptable and personally beneficial, mutually beneficial, or beneficial to others. By teaching those skills, we help kids learn new ways of thinking, new ways of feeling good, and new ways of behaving. When children are armed with an array of social skills, they are better able to take control of their lives and be successful. Whether you're a parent who wants your daughter to be a better problem-solver, or a counselor at a shelter who wants to help a runaway control his anger, teaching appropriate social skills is key.

Chapter 2 profiled the players involved in bullying, including the "typical" traits of each. Just as they differ in behaviors and attitudes, they also differ in the social skills they either possess or lack. There are many different social skills, too many to present in detail here. Individual circumstances may warrant specialized interventions, but generally speaking, the following skills can help bullies, bystanders, and victims break free of the behaviors that have trapped them in the bullying cycle. And the best part is that these skills can be taught by teachers during the school day and by parents in their homes.

Skills for Bullies

Bullies express aggressive or hostile behavior for a number of different reasons. Most are unable to understand others' feelings. Some simply cannot compromise. Rarely will you see a bully apologize or give anyone a compliment. Many show no empathy for their victims. Others simply want someone to notice them. For these bullies, a negative reaction from adults is better than no recognition at all. While there is a range of skills that can address each of these troubling characteristics, there are three in particular that offer a solid foundation for shaping an aggressive child's behavior toward more positive directions.

Accepting Differences

This skill is particularly important for youth who are prone to attacking others because they do not conform to whatever bullies believe to be "normal," whether in appearance, behavior, or belief. The first step in teaching bullies how to accept differences in others is to help them see how they are similar to or like others. After establishing a common ground, have bullies practice making positive statements about the uniqueness of others, or explain to them the concept of "just because you think it, you don't have to say it." Silence can sometimes be the best response. The third step is the Golden Rule test. To show bullies what it means to treat others as they would like to be treated, use a reverse role-play exercise. Have the bullies play the part of victims. Put bullies in the position of being verbally teased or physically intimidated because they are too short or too thin. Let them experience what it's like to be the butt of another person's mean attention.

Keep in mind that you should never use role reversal as a punishment to physically hurt or emotionally humiliate anyone. It's best if an adult role-plays the part of the bully. Make sure everyone understands that this is a perspective-taking exercise, an opportunity for bullies to see how uncomfortable their actions make others feel. Here are three steps children should follow when learning how to accept differences in others:

1. **Examine how you and the other person are alike.**
2. **Make positive comments or no comments about how the two of you are different.**
3. **Treat people of different races, sizes, and backgrounds the way you want to be treated.**

Expressing Empathy and Understanding for Others

Bullies are attuned to their own needs and impulses, but they have little regard for their victims' feelings. Getting them to be more empathetic won't happen overnight. Empathy has to be internalized, and that involves changing thoughts, feelings, and behaviors. Bullies have to first learn how to express empathy – even when they may not feel it – if they are going to internalize this skill.

Begin by teaching them how to recognize others' feelings through watching facial expressions and gestures, as well as listening to voice tone. Have them think about what feelings they might experience if they demonstrated similar expressions, gestures, or voice tones. Then have them express their concern by practicing saying statements such as, "I know you're unhappy about what just happened." Teach children to follow their expressions of concern with offers of help. Practice this skill by having children do the following:

1. **Listen closely to the other person's feelings.**
2. **Express empathy by saying, "I understand...."**

3. Demonstrate concern through words and actions.
4. Reflect back the other person's words by saying, "It seems like you're saying...."
5. Offer any help or assistance you can.

Apologizing

When bullies are caught, consequences rarely include making a sincere apology to their victims. It should. When bullies have to make an apology, it forces them to recognize that their actions were inappropriate. When victims accept an apology, they take the first step toward healing. But apologies sometimes have to come from more than just the bullies. If bystanders do nothing to help a bullying victim, they may also need to perform an act of contrition. Apologizing for inappropriate behavior is not always an easy thing to do. Here are basic steps you can teach bullies and/or bystanders to follow when making an apology:

1. Look at the person.
2. Using a sincere tone of voice, tell the person you would like to apologize.
3. Begin by saying, "I want to apologize for..." or "I'm sorry for...."
4. Clearly state what you did.
5. Take responsibility for everything you did wrong. Do not make excuses or give reasons for why you did what you did.
6. Say that you will try to avoid making the same mistake again.
7. If you took or damaged something, offer to replace or repair it.
8. Follow through with your offer.

Making an apology is often socially awkward for children, even when they follow the steps listed above. To ease their discomfort, a teacher, parent, or other adult should practice the skill with the bullies or bystanders before they approach the victims. In addition, adults should prepare and practice with victims the skill of accepting an apology, which involves looking at the person, not making sarcastic or angry comments or gestures, and thanking the person for apologizing.

Although we've focused our attention on three specific skills, it's important to note that self-control strategies are also helpful. Bullies have a hard time managing their emotions in certain situations. Helping them control their feelings before they go off on someone can involve techniques as straightforward as walking away, doing deep-breathing exercises, or using a journal to write down their thoughts and emotions.

Skills for Victims

Chapter 2 also highlighted two types of bullying victims. The vast majority of them are considered to be passive. They lack the ability and the confidence to deal with situations, and their submissive behavior toward bullies feeds the cycle of abuse. A smaller number of victims are considered provocative. They tend to annoy their peers, even adults, and they sometimes even intentionally open themselves up to abuse. Whether they're passive or provocative, here are three skills that will serve victims well.

Making Friends

A child doesn't have to try to be the most popular person at school, in the neighborhood, or on the team. Having just one or two good friends can be the difference between rarely being a victim and always being a target. Making friends is a skill, just like learning to ride a bike or playing the piano. While it might require more effort and practice for some, it can be learned. Here are strategies that can help anyone attract friends:

127

- **Develop a sense of humor.** Laughing at yourself or cracking jokes about your own shortcomings can take the edge off tense situations, and it can be disarming to anyone who may be thinking of starting trouble.

- **Respect the rights of others.** Learn how to listen to others without putting them down or trying to convince them that your opinion is the only one that matters.

- **Be kind and give sincere compliments to peers.** When you are kind to others, it's harder for them to be anything but kind to you.

FAMOUS NOW, A VICTIM THEN

"I was kind of a runty thing. And I liked to hang out with the girls. That annoyed the boys. So every day after school, they would throw me over the edge of the parking lot and roll me into the weeds. They weren't so much beatings as exercises in ritual humiliation. I knew the ritual had a form and a shape to it, and that it was far more efficient just to tumble down the hill in a satisfying way and then make my way up, rather than have to fight those guys to get back into the parking lot. Maybe they did it because they wanted a fight they could win. And my way of winning was to just hang in there."

– ACTOR HARRISON FORD
As quoted on www.fathom.com/feature/190179

- **Avoid "rejecting the rejecters."** If you're not chosen for the team or invited to the party, don't hate those who are. You only punish yourself when you carry hate or revenge inside of you.

- **Include others who are being left out** of a game or activity.

- **Be interested in what others are talking about,** rather than having others be interested in what you're talking about.

- **Notice what others are doing,** and ask them questions about it.

Asking for Help

Fear, embarrassment, and hopelessness are some of the emotions that explain why victims too often remain silent. Part of helping them overcome these barriers is making it clear that their privacy will be protected if they seek help, and they can trust that something positive will happen. We've explained how to create an environment that encourages communication and helps victims report abuse anonymously. But victims still have to do their part by taking the initiative to reach out to someone they trust, especially if what's happening to them is not obvious to others. Once they overcome their anxieties and believe that talking to someone will help, then teaching them how to ask for help becomes a matter of a few simple behavioral steps:

1. **Look at the person.**
2. **Ask the person if he or she has time to help you.**
3. **Clearly explain the kind of help that you need.**
4. **Thank the person for listening and assisting you.**

Stopping Negative Thoughts

If you think back to the "Fact or Fiction" Quiz in Chapter 1, you know that bullying is believed to be a contributing factor in adolescent suicides. The mental anguish experienced by some victims is just too overwhelming. But even those who don't resort to such an extreme measure must deal with bouts of depression and/or self-loathing. Unhealthy consequences usually result for anyone who wallows in negativity. It's especially important for victims not to fixate on all the bad things going on in their lives. You can help them take a different perspective by teaching them to do three things:

1. **Recognize negative thoughts when they come up,** especially thoughts of harming someone else or yourself.

2. **Say to yourself, "Everything will be okay,** and I'm not going to harm myself or anyone else." This is what we call "positive self-talk." When you focus on the good things going on in your life, even if it's something as small as a victory by your favorite sports team or buying a new CD released by your favorite band, you remember that not everything in your life is bad.

3. **Find a trusted adult** (counselor, teacher, parent, older sibling, relative) and talk about your thoughts and feelings.

Stopping negative thoughts can be a difficult task for victims who are feeling depressed and anxious. Imagine telling a chocolate lover not to think about chocolate-dipped strawberries when he's standing in the middle of a berry patch. The first thing he's likely to think about is chocolate. For victims of bullying, getting them to stop dwelling on negative thoughts can be done using distraction techniques. This can involve anything from having them read an entertaining book or play a game of cards to helping prepare a meal or engaging in a conversation about movies or music. It's hard to maintain negative thought patterns when the mind has to concentrate on something completely different, such as playing a game or finishing a task.

Skills for Bystanders

When you can motivate bystanders to help victims, you create an environment where respect and tolerance, not disrespect and indifference, are the norm. Young people who witness bullying or have knowledge of incidents don't always exactly know how to stand up to social pressure, comfort victims, or even discreetly report students' behavior. Fortunately, these are all skills that they can learn.

Resisting Negative Peer Pressure

This is difficult, especially for older adolescents who are more interested in fitting in than standing apart. You can make it more likely that they will intervene by teaching them simple verbal responses. Statements such as "No" or "Hey, he [the victim] doesn't deserve that. Leave him alone," can be helpful. Another strategy to standing up against bullies is to divert their attention to something else. Suggest doing something fun, like playing a game, going to a movie, or anything that might change their focus. When all else fails, bystanders need to leave the situation and report what's going on. When teaching children how to resist peer pressure, have them practice these steps:

1. **Look at the person.**
2. **Use a calm voice.**
3. **Say clearly that you do not want to participate.**
4. **Suggest something else to do.**
5. **If necessary, continue to say "No."**
6. **Leave the situation.**

Reporting Others' Behavior

Reporting should be the primary strategy for youth who confront bullying situations that are too difficult or dangerous for them to personally intervene. For older kids, reporting can often be difficult because the environment makes it socially unacceptable. If the cost to an adolescent for exposing a bully or a bullying incident is retaliation, he or she won't pay that price. Regardless of how supportive the environment is, every child needs this skill. How you teach it, however, will differ according to the child's age. Young children in elementary or middle school will benefit from learning the In/Out Rule. This rule helps them sort out when they need to come forward and when they shouldn't. Here are the steps to following the In/Out Rule:

1. **Think about what is happening.**
2. **Are you thinking about telling to get someone "In" or "Out" of trouble? "In" trouble is when you tattle for no special reason. "Out" of trouble is when you want to help someone to avoid getting hurt.**
3. **If your answer is "In" trouble, don't tell.**
4. **If your answer is "Out" of trouble, then tell an adult right away.**

With adolescents or teens, teach these steps:

1. **Recognize when others are being hurt, physically or emotionally.**
2. **Ask yourself if you can safely intervene. If you can, do.**
3. **If you cannot, stay calm and find an adult to talk to or privately write down what you are reporting.**
4. **Whether writing or talking, be specific about who did what, where, and to whom.**

Showing Concern for Someone Who's Been Hurt

Some children who watch others being bullied often feel regret and shame afterwards because they did nothing to help.

But help can come in many forms, at many times. Ideally, we want bystanders to intervene immediately. But when they don't, they can still play a positive role by using this skill. Here's what it looks like:

1. **Calmly talk to the victim one-on-one or ask him or her to join you and your friends.**

2. **Express concern by saying something like, "I saw what they did and heard what they said to you. It's mean and you don't deserve to be treated like that."**

3. **Invite the person into some positive activities with you and your friends.**

4. **Find common interests and positive things to share and say to the person.**

All of these skills can be modified to fit the age or developmental level of the children you're dealing with. Keep in mind that learning these skills requires practice. Most children will have to be reminded of these skills and their individual steps repeatedly before they master them and can apply them in their everyday lives.

Teaching Methods

Now that you've learned how social skills can help shape the behaviors of bullies, victims, and bystanders in positive ways, let's discuss how best to introduce and teach those skills. We recommend three teaching methods that are fundamentally sound and easy to understand. They are pre-teaching positive skills, correcting inappropriate behaviors, and offering effective praise. (We'll also discuss the importance of using consequences.) These teaching methods are very similar to how a teacher introduces a new academic lesson to his class or how a coach explains an opponent's game plan to her team.

Pre-Teaching Positive Social Skills

With this approach, you teach kids new skills or behaviors that will prepare them before they face another new or difficult situation. For example, do you think it is better to correct and teach a child not to touch a hot stove after she has burned her hand on it, or to teach her ahead of time that touching a stove can hurt her and that she shouldn't go near it? Obviously, prevention is the best answer. When children know what is expected of them, and have the opportunity to prepare, they will be more successful.

Teaching skills proactively is especially important when you work with victims who have had difficulty dealing with bullies in the past. Here are the three steps to pre-teaching a skill or behavior and an example of how it looks:

1. **Describe what you would like.**

    "Stephen, the next time Darius makes fun of your glasses or calls you four-eyes, say to him, 'So?' or 'Well, they're better to see you with,' and then walk away."

2. **Give a reason.**

    "If you stand up to Darius and act like what he says doesn't bother you, he probably will stop teasing you and move on to something else."

3. **Practice.**

    "Let's pretend that I'm teasing you. What are you going to say and do?" (Stephen says 'So?' and then walks away.) "That's great Stephen! It's important to know how to stand up for yourself."

Before kids can do what you want, they must first know what is expected. By giving them a reason for why they should act in certain ways, they can see and understand what the future benefits might be for them. Practicing also raises their confidence and sets them up for success instead of failure.

Using Consequences

Consequences help kids make the connection between what they do and what happens as a result of their choices or actions. **Positive consequences** should be given after a particular appropriate behavior to increase the likelihood that the behavior will be repeated. **Negative consequences** should be given after a particular inappropriate behavior to decrease the possibility of it happening again. Positive or negative consequences will be effective only if you follow some basic principles:

- Consequences must be **important** to youth, otherwise there will be little effect on behavior.

- Consequences must be delivered as **immediately** as possible to make a clear connection and understanding between the behavior and the consequence.

- Consequences must be **appropriate** for the behavior. Do not burden children with excessive negative consequences for the small stuff. Neither should you ignore or under-reward them for making the best choices.

- Consequences must be **consistent.** If you address a certain behavior on Monday, you shouldn't ignore that same behavior on Friday. Being consistent also means that you don't treat kids differently. The ADHD child should be praised for his or her efforts and good behavior as much as the athletically or academically gifted child.

The consequences you use to reinforce or discourage certain behaviors can be unlimited, but they should never include harming a child's physical or emotional well-being. For example, educators might reward good behaviors with positive notes home to parents, verbal praise, or extra playing time for children on sports teams. Negative consequences could include verbal reprimands, staying after school, phone calls to parents, or loss of playing time. For parents, positive consequences used in the home might involve verbal praise, extended curfews, or greater independence. Consequences for misbehaviors might involve restricted phone or computer use, loss of driving privileges, or restrictions on the amount of time spent with friends. Consequences should be used to reinforce the behaviors you want to see again or to discourage bad behaviors from being repeated.

Correcting Inappropriate Behavior

No matter how proactive you are in teaching kids appropriate expectations and using positive social skills, they will test limits and do things they shouldn't. One of the reasons bullies are the way they are is because they have learned that being aggressive gets them what they want. Rarely has anyone ever consistently corrected their behavior or taught them more appropriate behaviors or skills. That's why teachers, parents, and others have to recognize and respond to misbehaviors in more assertive, constructive ways. Correcting inappropriate behavior is similar to the pre-teaching method discussed earlier. In corrective teaching, the focus is on building relationships, describing the behaviors, and using negative consequences. Within each of these concepts are component steps that give structure to the teaching process. Here are those component steps and their descriptions:

Building a Relationship

- **Give initial praise or express empathy** – Begin corrective teaching in a positive way. It lets the child know that you care enough to help. It also is a way to calm emotions so he or she can work out the problem and think of ways to fix it. Try to recognize the child for some positive behavior he or she demonstrates, such as listening to you or calming down. You might praise the child by saying, "Jared, thanks for looking at me when I'm talking." An empathy statement might be, "Jared, I know it can be hard to keep some comments to yourself." Brevity is essential. If you talk too long, kids tune out.

Describing the Behavior

- **Describe the inappropriate behavior** – Tell the child what he or she did wrong or failed to do; for example, "Jared, you made a comment that's not okay in this classroom. Remember the Airport Rule? It says, 'We will not say negative things about others. If we do, we'll be detained.'" Keep your comments simple, brief, and focused on the behavior rather than on emotions or the individual.

- **Describe an appropriate behavior** – Give a simple explanation of a behavior that the child can use in place of the inappropriate behavior he or she demonstrated. Using Jared as an example, you might say, "Jared, when someone says an answer aloud in class, you should either say nothing or make a positive comment."

- **Give a rationale** – Explain why the child should change his or her behavior. For younger children, this reason should focus on how they will personally benefit from using a new behavior. Older adolescents need to know how engaging in more positive behaviors will

be good for them and/or others. For Jared, the rationale might sound like this: "When we encourage our
classmates, all of us will feel safe to express ourselves
without fear of being made fun of."

Giving a Consequence

- **Give a consequence** – It is important when giving
  consequences that the child understands that his or her
  behavior earned the consequence and that he or she is
  responsible for that behavior. Avoid statements such as,

CONSEQUENCES THAT ARE OUTSIDE THE BOX

In education settings, detentions or in-school suspensions
are common consequences for children caught bullying
others. But that approach often denies children a chance
to learn some important skills. In fact, many students tell
us detention is really no big deal to them. Some spend
their time taking naps while others daydream.

For students who bully, a more constructive consequence
is one that teaches them about empathy and understanding. Here are four "outside-the-box" consequences that
emphasize teaching and learning rather than punishing
and forgetting:

- Participate in a community service project,
  under proper supervision, that helps others.

- Read articles on bullying, then write an essay
  or give an oral presentation.

- Write an apology.

- Read to or be a mentor to younger children.

"I'm taking away…" or "I'm never letting you…." A better approach is to say something like, "Because you said hurtful words, you lose the privilege of…." You want to reinforce the idea that the child's behavior is the cause of the negative consequence. You may find that the child perceives the attention and time you spend one-on-one correcting his or her behavior to be part of the negative consequence. That's okay. Unwanted attention from an adult can be an incentive for the child to improve his or her behavior. In addition to losing a privilege, the child needs to apologize to the victim(s) as part of the consequence.

- **Practice** – In most situations, it's a good idea to have the child practice making an apology before he or she faces the victim. Again, we'll use Jared as an example. Here's what you might say: "Since you made that comment about Jacinda, you will apologize to her after class. You can write down for me, or tell me, what you're going to say to Jacinda before you apologize to make sure that you feel comfortable with your apology."

- **Praise and follow up** – Always finish the interaction with a positive statement. For example, you can say, "Thank you for listening to me, Jared, and for working through this. I'll meet you at the end of class before you apologize to Jacinda." Always recognize a child's efforts to learn or practice a new behavior. This can be done any time a youth responds to teaching in a positive way.

When giving consequences, your voice tone and physical gestures should be calm. Model behaviors for children that show them how to deal appropriately with negative situations. In addition, the consequences should reflect the severity of the incident. Severe consequences for mild misbehaviors or small consequences for serious infractions can produce unintended results. Ideally, you will look at the frequency, intensity, and duration of the behavior to determine the appropriate response.

If you're correcting children because you saw or heard them bullying others, it's important to record what happened and how you intervened. Documentation involves noting the who, what, where, and when of an incident, as well as what consequences were given. This is especially important for teachers or support staff who work with dozens of children every day. Simply relying on memory can be problematic when there are many names and faces to remember and you have to explain a not-so-recent bullying incident to a frustrated administrator or irate parent.

We recommend that you **praise** children **four times** as often as you correct them.

Writing down what happened and how you responded allows you to compare notes with other staff to see if there are any common factors (same individuals, same locations, same circumstances) between what you saw and what they've experienced. Documenting your intervention efforts also offers a measure of protection from parents who may come to school angry that their child was bullied and mad because you did nothing to stop it. Proper documentation can show that you were aware of the incident and took measures that were helpful to the bully and the victim.

Offering Effective Praise

Everyone appreciates receiving praise. For young people, it's the key to healthy emotions. Praise is also a powerful motivator. Unfortunately, despite all of its positive qualities, praise is not used as often as it should be. Criticism comes easily. Zeroing in on the good things kids do, even acknowledging the absence of negative behaviors, gets overlooked. To create a healthy environment where bullying cannot flourish, adults must praise the positive skills and good behaviors that bullies, victims, and bystanders demonstrate. When victims assert themselves in positive ways, their efforts should be applauded. When bystanders act as a positive influence, they should be encouraged. Even bullies can't be mean all the time. When they show respect, concern, or empathy, they should be praised.

Here are a few guidelines for making praise work:

- **Praise the behavior in a way that children understand.**

  If you use only general phrases such as, "Excellent" or "Great," young people may not understand exactly what you're happy about. It's best to specifically describe the behavior you want to see repeated. Say things such as, "You did a great job of involving all your classmates in the project. You listened to their ideas and always thanked them for their input." Specificity helps children know what behaviors you approve of and want to see again.

- **Be enthusiastic!**
  Express your satisfaction enthusiastically. A pleasant voice, a thumbs-up, or a clap of hands expresses emotion and shows children that you feel good about what happened.

- **Give praise at an appropriate time and in ways that are appealing to youth.**
  Usually, praise should be given immediately after a positive action. However, there may be situations when

it's better to wait. Some kids don't like to be praised in front of others; it embarrasses them. Then there are kids who love the spotlight, and want public praise. Know your kids, and offer a variety of praise that is meaningful and personal to each.

- **Move to more general praise after a skill is mastered.** When children demonstrate behaviors or skills frequently, too much specific praise can be nonreinforcing or irritating, or come off as condescending. In these situations, you can show your appreciation by pointing out their overall qualities – "You're a team player" or "Great job today!"

When you use praise with children, you're actually modeling how to notice and express appreciation. Your praise actually encourages kids to be pleasant to others. Praise also reflects what you value. The more you call attention to words and actions that embody respect, tolerance, acceptance, and friendship, the more rewards you will reap. In fact, we recommend that you praise children four times as often as you correct them. If you really want to see improvement in your children's behavior, especially bullies, you must acknowledge the positive things they do.

Giving Kids a Reason to Change

Those who simply hope that bullies will magically stop being aggressive, and victims will stop being doormats, and bystanders will stop being cheerleaders, are destined for disappointment. These are not phases that children will outgrow. When bullies get their needs met through aggression, they have no reason to change. When victims remain passive, unable to assert themselves, they will always be targets for manipulation and victimization. When bystanders encourage bullies and ignore victims, they contribute to a climate of fear and anxiety that is just as threatening for them as it is for others.

The previous chapter asked what a reasonable response to bullying problems is. The answer is aggressive prevention coupled with consistent intervention. Prevention involves rules, which bring order to a child's daily activities, and procedures, which guide his or her actions. The third component is teaching skills and behaviors, which help a child deal with aggression and bullying. Intervention also means a child has to experience consequences for his or her actions, whether positive or negative.

As you assess the situation in your classrooms, youth clubs, programs, or families, determine which of these elements can be strengthened or expanded to produce a safer, more enriching environment. Bullies, victims, and bystanders can't be expected to solve this problem on their own. You have to correct, guide, teach, console, and encourage them.

chapter

By **Bridget Barnes**
Michael Handwerk, Ph.D.

Parents as Advocates in the School and Home

"Next year, I will be documenting everything. I will phone the school every time he is called a name or threatened. And I will hire a lawyer. I have put this off and have made my son suffer. Well, no more."

"Bullying is alive and well, with teachers saying, 'Suck it up,' making it the victim's problem, making the victim the bad guy."

■ ■ ■

These comments from frustrated parents, as reported in one local newspaper,[1] exemplify one of the most distressing issues we encounter when dealing with bullying: the animosity and distrust that divide parents and teachers. Because kids spend so much of their day in education settings, school officials are often the first to bring bullying problems to parents' attention. But it's not always appreciated. Just hearing the word "bullying" conjures up a whole set of emotions that can easily lead to friction between the home and the school. Whether a child is a victim or an aggressor, the perceptions and reactions from adults are often unpredictable.

When a bullying incident is reported, some parents see the school as the enemy and are quick to blame staff for allowing their children to be mistreated. Other parents (of bullies) blame the school for overreacting to "innocent" behavior or being too "politically correct." Then there are different perceptions from school officials. There are educators who lay blame on parents who they feel are too protective of their overly sensitive children. Other educators blame parents who they feel are too lax with discipline and too tolerant of too much. In the end, we see adults reacting with a mix of sadness, fear, anxiety, anger, disappointment, indifference, and, occasionally, relief. (Parents have actually told us that they felt better after hearing their child was the bully, not the victim. For them, having a "tough" kid was better than having a "weak" one.)

In our experience, we've seen parents react way too defensively, just as we've seen teachers and administrators do the same. All of this sometimes aggressive posturing between adults only exacerbates the problem. With bullying, the focus has to be on dealing with the behavior of youth, not questioning the motives of other adults. The previous chapters focused a lot on what teachers, coaches, and others can do in their schools, clubs, and organizations. Now, we turn our attention to parents, and how they can be a positive influence for their children at home and outside the home.

Working with Schools

There is a well-known saying that "every community gets the schools it deserves." High parental involvement brings quality education, and apathy brings mediocrity. While this is a simplistic way to look at things, the fact remains that lack of parental involvement reduces the quality of a school and weakens the watchdog factor that prevents problems from escalating out of control. Sometimes, parents might feel like it's too big of a hassle to get involved. Considering the stakes, however, it is certainly worth the effort.

As a parent, you don't want your first conversation with teachers or administrators to be about your child's behavior problem. If you don't know them and they don't know you, it can be very easy to dismiss each other. And if you immediately start making threats or accusations when there is a problem involving your child, you may antagonize the very people who are in the best position to help. You might be hurting your child as well; if teachers and administrators form a bad opinion of you, it may affect how they perceive your child. It shouldn't, but we're all human. Rather than waiting until problems develop, we recommend getting involved early. Parental involvement with schools has many benefits and is not as daunting as you may think. Here are three ways to cultivate a relationship with your children's school and enhance your communication efforts before and after a problem develops.

Use the Four A's

This proactive strategy helps you enlist the support of staff **before** problems arise. The A's stand for **A**ppreciation, **A**wareness, **A**vailability, and **A**lliance. Here is how you can use each area to build a positive, working relationship with teachers or administrators:

- **Appreciation** – Take the time to say "Thank you." Whether you communicate through a phone call, an e-mail, or a handwritten note, any kind word can energize teachers and give them a boost of confidence to deal with their daily challenges, including bullying. Let them know that you value their work, and that you understand that they have to deal with hundreds of different kids from all different kinds of families.

- **Awareness** – Let your presence be known. Attend parent-teacher conferences and go to open houses. Take advantage of volunteer opportunities and find out what the teachers and other staff members are doing to promote respect and keep kids safe.

- **Availability** – Respond to contacts and requests. If a teacher calls to report on your child's behavior, take the report seriously. Agree to meet with the teacher or an administrator if asked. Most educators will not take the time to call you unless they feel it's truly important.

- **Alliance** – See yourself as part of the school community, not as an adversary or passive observer. An issue as serious as bullying cannot be addressed only by you or only by the school. You have to work with the school to develop anti-bullying policies and reinforce behavior expectations. Likewise, school officials have to be open to your concerns, especially if your child is a victim, a bully, or a bystander.

We realize that having a relationship with your child's teachers and establishing regular communication with the school does not always mean that friction won't develop. If you're not satisfied with a teacher's initial response to a bullying incident, share your concerns with him or her first. Keep a record of your conversations and contacts with the teacher. If the problem persists or seems to be worsening, then you need to take the next step and speak with a principal or school psychologist. The key thing to remember, especially if your child is being bullied, is that you want it to stop. If you are hostile toward the person or people who need to intervene on your behalf when you're not there, intervention is less likely to occur. You need to make friends at your child's school, not enemies. You need to focus on solutions, not dwell on who is to blame.

Find an Educational Mentor

If your child is constantly having problems with a bully (or if he or she is the bully), and a teacher or administrator is less than helpful, consider enlisting an educational mentor for your child. A mentor is first and foremost an advocate for your child. Ideally, it would be someone in the school, such as a teacher, paraprofessional, or helper whom your child knows and likes. Educational mentors are often called on to help kids who struggle with academic subjects, but they can also assist with issues that impede learning, such as bullying. The mentor can work with your child one-on-one during the school day to teach skills, target weaknesses, and build on strengths. A mentor can also act as a liaison. He or she knows the school system well and can ease any friction that exists between parents and school staff. For example, a mentor can represent your child during parent/teacher meetings and perhaps offer a perspective that neither you nor the teacher can see.

Use Behavior Cards and School Notes

A behavior card or school note enables and improves communication after a bullying problem has been identified. Have your child's teacher use the card or note as a way to document the kinds of interactions your child has with other kids. The card **must** be used in conjunction with other intervention efforts, including the teaching of social skills, such as those described in

the previous chapter. The card is another channel of communication between the school and the home to track and measure
the effectiveness of your intervention efforts. Here are examples
of the behaviors or interactions that you would include on a
behavior card if your child was using bullying behaviors:

• Bossed someone around	YES/NO
• Bothered or annoyed someone	YES/NO
• Picked a fight with someone	YES/NO
• Was rude to or disrespected someone	YES/NO
• Called someone names; put someone down	YES/NO
• Criticized or treated someone as though he or she was weird, awkward, or different	YES/NO

You can use the behavior card if your child is a victim, too.
You simply reverse the focus of the statements. For example,
"Bossed someone around" becomes "Bossed around by someone," or "Was rude to or disrespected someone" becomes "Was
disrespected by someone." Think of the card or note as an
incident report that teachers can fill out on a daily or weekly basis.
The card reflects the observations of the teacher. Be prepared
for possible resistance, however. A common complaint parents
hear from teachers is that they don't have time to fill out a card
for your child. If that's the case, simplify the note so that it's easy
for teachers to use. Identify one or two key behaviors that need
to occur or that you are concerned about. For instance, the form
could report the number of times your child was picked on in a
day or week. Use a numerical reference (1, 2, 3) or words (never,
sometimes, always). If that's not doable, ask the teacher to write

down his or her observations in one or two sentences. It could be as simple as, "Saw your child sharing and cooperating with another child." Again, the card supplements intervention efforts. Tracking the problem won't mean anything if you're not working with your child to develop healthy relationship skills that he or she can use in daily activities. For more suggestions on successfully using behavior cards, see page 152.

The Four A's, educational mentors, and behavior cards or notes are ways to enhance communication efforts and focus everyone's attention on solving the problem. Remember, you can't know what's going on at school unless you ask or someone tells you. Likewise, you can't express your concerns unless someone at the school is listening. There has to be an attempt at beginning and continuing communication. As a parent, establishing an effective dialogue with your child's school is the most critical step.

Working with Your Child and Watching Yourself

Beginning in Chapter 6, we presented ways for all of the stakeholders – both in education settings and other youth-related organizations – to act in partnership with one another to create healthy, positive environments. As a parent, you know what your relationship has to be like with teachers, administrators, and others. But you also need to have a positive relationship with your child. Let's look at what you can do to help your child if he or she acts like a bully, prefers to be an unhelpful bystander, or is being bullied.

When Your Child Acts Like a Bully

Many parents fail to realize that their attitudes and behaviors are often mimicked by their children. Kids take into the world the things they learn and are exposed to inside their homes.

THREE ESSENTIAL RULES FOR USING BEHAVIOR CARDS

1. Before a behavior card is used, there must be a meeting of the parent(s), student, teacher, and member of the administrative team (principal or assistant principal). During the meeting, the child has to be seen AND heard. You don't want to have a meeting where the adults do all the talking and dictating. The child needs to help identify situations and behaviors that cause him or her trouble. You can help your child recognize these situations by teaching the SODAS method, which we describe at the end of this chapter. In addition, expectations should be clarified and an agreement made on how the card will be used, including the kinds of follow-up procedures that will be done to see how well the card is working.

2. A behavior card is meant to be a positive tool, not a weapon for punishment. The card should also have balance, meaning it should highlight good and bad behaviors. Using the card will be completely ineffective if a teacher only says, "That's bullying. I'm marking your card." Success depends on the teacher praising good behaviors, correcting the bad, teaching social skills, and providing appropriate feedback to parents so they too can teach and reinforce appropriate behaviors at home.

3. A behavior card is a short-term intervention strategy. The card should be phased out and replaced with more specific verbal praise and communication once the child consistently demonstrates the positive behaviors you're trying to teach and reinforce.

If you humiliate or put down your children, they learn how to hurt others emotionally and will likely do the same thing in relationships where they have more power. If you look the other way or remain silent every time something bad goes on in your home, your children will likely do the same when they witness bullying situations. If you allow an older child to constantly boss around or threaten a younger sibling, two things are likely to happen. The older child will start thinking that he or she can act that same way toward anyone, especially those who are not as strong, and the younger child will try to find an outlet for his or her frustration. The younger child may adopt the role of permanent victim or try to victimize others in the same way he or she was abused, which is similar to the bully-victim concept introduced in Chapter 2. If you want to know why your child is acting like a bully, you may only have to look in the mirror or listen to your own words. Have you ever responded to your child's aggression with statements like these?

"I would have done the same thing!"

Your child takes advantage of someone. Maybe he hit a classmate. Maybe she retaliated against a rival by starting a vicious rumor. If your only response to bad behavior is to applaud it, or say that you would have done the same thing, you're sending a bad message. One of the most powerful teaching tools you have is modeling the behavior you want your children to learn. You have to "walk the talk," and be the person of integrity that you want your children to become.

Everything you do, and don't do, sends a message to your kids about your values. Be sure your messages are about doing the right thing, even when it is hard to do. When you slip (and all of us do), do what you want your children to do when they make a mistake – be accountable, apologize sincerely, and work to do better.

"Did you win?"

Most responsible parents do not intentionally teach their children to behave like bullies. But they sometimes can reinforce bullying behavior. This happens when you choose to encourage, reward, or acknowledge your child's aggressive behavior as being entirely appropriate. By reinforcement, we don't necessarily mean a pat on the back or a "Good job!" Parents can reinforce bad behavior, often inadvertently, with their silence. Saying and doing nothing after your child acts out inappropriately is, ironically, the loudest and clearest way to tell your child that what he or she did was okay.

Author and consultant Michele Borba advises parents in her book, *Parents Do Make a Difference,* to address any uncaring behavior they see from their child, even behavior that wouldn't be described as bullying but just insensitive. The idea is to "plant the seeds of empathy." She uses the acronym **CARE** to illustrate how parents should respond:

- **C**all attention to the uncaring behavior.

- **A**sk your child, "How would you feel?"

- **R**ecognize the consequence of the action.
  (Ask questions that make your child see how his or her actions made another person feel.)

- **E**xpress and explain your disapproval of the behavior.

Remember, difficult behavior problems sometimes can be avoided if parents are able and willing to deal with the little issues that can lead up to the big problems. Parents simply cannot remain silent. You need to make it explicitly clear to your child that you will not tolerate bullying behavior. Don't just make comments such as, "Don't let me catch you doing that again," or "How many times have I said bullying is wrong!" Those are just empty threats if your child never experiences any negative consequences for his or her behavior. There need to be consequences, but they should never be violent. You don't want to send the message that "Might is right."

"I can't do anything – they see it on television and in music videos. It's everywhere!"

It can be tempting to absolve yourself of any responsibility by blaming a culture you believe celebrates violence and demonizes compassion. But do you really think cultural messages have more influence on your children's attitudes and behaviors than you do? You might – if you allow the culture to be your children's primary teacher. If your children see and hear only the media's definition of concepts such as friendship, tolerance, responsibility, and respect, then their perceptions may be warped. Some TV shows, films, video games, and music videos are notorious for their warped interpretation of certain values. But even if you took all those things away from your kids, they would still be exposed to some harmful or contradictory messages from the environment, including peers. Rather than throwing your hands up in the air and tuning out, choose to tune in. Be a filter and provide a counterview or balance to the messages reaching your children. Talk openly about values and character issues, including fairness and responsibility. Help them to evaluate media messages more critically so they don't assume everything they see or hear is the "truth" or is "reality." Chapter 11 shows you how to help your children become media literate and disrupt the constant flow of mindless media into their lives. Encourage participation in community service projects that affirm the values you cherish and want your children to learn. When it comes to establishing values, beliefs, and character in your children, the most powerful tool you have is yourself.

Remember, bullies generally suffer worse outcomes in the short term and long term than victims. Parents who support their children's bullying behaviors are rolling the dice with their children's possibilities for success in later life.

When Your Child Is a Bystander

Being the bystander can be as traumatizing as being the victim. Many parents don't realize the anxiety and stress bystanders experience because those are scars not easily seen. Imagine witnessing someone getting humiliated or beaten day in and day out. The hateful words and behaviors can take a deep emotional and mental toll on anyone, especially children. Bystanders can – and are – getting hurt from the backlash and turmoil that's unleashed by aggressive and hostile individuals and environments. With that in mind, here are three important points parents should consider if they want to help a child who is exposed to bullying situations:

- Find opportunities to teach your child how to avoid being a do-nothing bystander.

- Think of ways to address your child's needs when he or she witnesses bullying.

- Reinforce your child's ability to break the bystander "mode."

Find opportunities to teach your child how to avoid being a do-nothing bystander.

The next time you sit down as a family to watch a movie or TV show, or even read a book or magazine, pay attention to the characters depicted on the page or screen. Point out to your children the characters who, by their words or actions, play the part of a bystander. Use those characters to help your children recognize what it means to be a bystander and how the actions of bystanders can have good or bad consequences. If a character's actions were hurtful to others, ask your children what the character could have done differently to be a positive influence. Likewise, if a character comes to the defense of someone who is being taken advantage of physically or emotionally, try to relate that situation to what goes on in your children's lives. Ask them what they could do (or have done) when they see others being bullied. Talk about actions (reporting the behavior to an adult, confronting the bully, and/or comforting the victim) that are both responsible and respectful.

For some parents, the best teaching moments aren't found in a book or movie, instead they are found in their living rooms, kitchens, and backyards. For example, parents often share with us their frustration with children who instigate, encourage, or watch fights between other siblings. If you have children who are less than helpful, you should teach them how to be more responsive in positive ways. You might teach them how to ask for help from an adult, how to use their words to break up a fight, or how to remove themselves from the situation. Here's how one parent explained his expectations to his son:

> A study of more than 1,200 4-year-olds found that those who had greater exposure to television were more likely to become bullies later on in school. However, toddlers whose parents provided more emotional support, such as reading to them and going on outings, were less likely to become bullies.
>
> Archives of *Pediatrics and Adolescent Medicine,* 2005

"Spencer, I want you to learn how to be more helpful when your brothers are fighting. The next time you see them going at each other, I want you to say, 'Jackson and Ryan, stop fighting and come with me. We'll get Mom or Dad to solve this problem so you two won't get into any more trouble.' Whatever you do Spencer, don't encourage your brothers to fight. When you act responsibly, I can see you're becoming more mature, which means you can have more freedom to do some of the things you enjoy. Do you understand what I'm asking you to do, Spencer?"

In this example, notice how the parent managed to explain his expectations, describe the specific behaviors he wanted to see from his son, and give a reason or rationale why his son should do what he asked. This is very similar to the pre-teaching social skills method described in the previous chapter. In this case, if the son meets the expectations set by his father, he will be rewarded with more freedoms. Likewise, if he does not, a negative consequence (more restrictions) will result. Motivating children to change their behaviors requires acknowledging and praising the actions that you want to see again and correcting those behaviors that you don't want to see.

Think of ways to address your child's needs when he or she witnesses bullying.

Children who witness acts of bullying sometimes compare their experiences to that of a deer frozen in a car's headlights. They are paralyzed in the moment. This paralysis can be caused by fear, indifference, confusion, or a combination of factors. Some kids say they feel a great deal of shame afterwards for having done nothing. This is what we call "bystander silence." Some kids try to push their feelings aside, but emotions have a funny way of seeping out eventually. As a parent, you should be mindful of changes in your child's behavior. If he or she is usually cooperative at school but suddenly becomes more defiant, this could be a sign that he or she is suffering "bystander silence."

When parents are tuned into their children's odd emotional swings or outbursts, or notice they are being overly fearful or emotionally numb at home or school, they can better address their children's needs. Make a point to check in with your child each day about his or her experiences. Ask questions in a way that encourages your child to share a story with you.

For example, you could say to your child, "Tell me about something really cool that happened to you or someone you know today." Then say, "Tell me about something that wasn't so cool that happened to you or to someone you know today." Don't be too quick to judge what your child shares with you. Instead, listen, show empathy, and provide help if needed.

Reinforce your child's ability to break the bystander "mode."

Breaking the bystander mode isn't easy because it's often reinforced by peers or often goes unnoticed by adults. Rarely does a bystander receive a negative consequence from a parent or teacher. In fact, such behavior is usually seen as socially acceptable.

Perhaps the most important reason why it is difficult to break the bystander mode is that bad behavior gets more attention. If your child acts outrageously or uses foul language, you're going to notice. Bystanders are often overlooked by adults, including parents.

Here are three simple ideas for reinforcing your children when they don't engage in bystander behavior:

- **Praise them.** It sounds simple, doesn't it? Well, it is. Kids like praise just like everyone else. So when they make the right decision to either walk away or quietly get some help, praise them.

- **Set up a "clue" word.** No kid wants to be labeled a snitch. Most would rather take a beating. Give your child a way to let a trusted adult know when bullying behavior is occurring by coming up with a gesture or clue word. It's then up to the adult to act accordingly while keeping the youth's name out of it.

- **Reward them.** Recognize your child's efforts to change his or her behavior. Even if the improvement is small, it's important to acknowledge the small steps so that more steps will be taken.

If you want your children to be a positive influence in their environment and in their relationships, you need to show them how. Don't assume they'll know what to do or will always do what's right. You have to make your kids understand that when they do nothing, they are as guilty of hurting victims as the bullies are.

When Your Child Is Bullied

Victims of bullies can take steps to better protect themselves and make living with a bully easier. This includes learning how to be more assertive and confident. However, that's sometimes easier said than done. As a parent, you need to help your child find the courage and the confidence to overcome feelings of worthlessness and victimization. Here are some suggestions to help your child deal with a bully and stop being a victim.

Identify the situations in which bullying is likely to occur.

Avoiding certain individuals or areas is a strategy your child should use. But to do it, your child needs to be aware of the circumstances that might put him or her at risk. For example, one young boy was bullied whenever he played football with a group of older youth during an aftercare program. His mother was quite distressed, but taking him out of the program was not an option. Fortunately in this case, there was a simpler solution. The aftercare program had dozens of activities for the boy to participate in, so he didn't have to play football. For a few weeks, he hung out with other kids and played cards and did art projects, and he kept his distance from the boys who had bullied him. That was enough time for the situation to cool down. After a while, the older youth forgot all about him. Understand that there are going to be times when your child can't avoid certain situations or people. That is why the best strategy always includes teaching skills and assertive behaviors.

Teach appropriate responses to bullying.

If your child reacts emotionally to bullying, either by crying or getting angry, he or she only invites more torment. Therefore, it's important to help your child minimize the reaction he or she has to bullying. Two strategies that we've discussed earlier deserve a second mention: humor and positive self-talk.

Humor doesn't mean having a whole stand-up routine. A one-liner or little quip can interject humor into an otherwise threatening situation and make it seem like your child isn't bothered at all by what the bully says or does. For example, a red-haired girl was repeatedly taunted by classmates who made comments such as, "I'd rather be dead than red on the head!" Every day for a week, the young girl went home crying. Instead of calling the school and demanding immediate punishment for the tormentors, her parents talked to her about what she could say in response to those comments, and then had her practice saying those words. The next time a classmate said, "I'd rather be dead than red on the head," the little girl responded, "Yeah, me too. Oh wait. I am red on the head." She said it with a smile and a laugh. Her reply not only showed assertiveness, but it told the bullies that the reason they picked on her wasn't going to work anymore. When victims stop giving bullies emotional responses, oftentimes the bullying stops.

Positive self-talk is another strategy for keeping emotions under control. Essentially, this is a mental conversation that can help victims through difficult moments. You might teach your child to repeat a self-affirming phrase such as, "I am a good person, and things will get better." Whatever a victim can do to keep from crying or having an emotional blowup in front of the bully is ideal. Another benefit of positive self-talk is that it can lift a depressed child's spirits. Victims need to find ways to see a silver lining; otherwise, they can be consumed by feelings of hopelessness.

Increase your child's social network.

The more isolated your child is, the more likely he or she will continue to be bullied. Increasing your child's social network means helping him or her develop friendships and more peer relationships. **This does not mean** signing your child up for every conceivable club or program. If all you're doing is putting him or her in more activities, you're just providing more opportunities for victimization. You have to teach your child how to make friends (see Chapter 6), initiate conversations, and be part of group activities. Something as basic as starting a conversation can be the key to success. For example, if a child is being rejected or ignored by a group, it might be because he or she is taking the wrong approach. Instead of focusing on what he or she wants or has, the child should ask questions that focus on the interests of the kids he or she wants to connect with.

Avoid remarks such as "Toughen up" or "Stand up and be a man."

Pat phrases are meaningless. In addition to the shame and embarrassment many victims feel, they also experience guilt because they are not living up to parental expectations. Victims can interpret statements like these as confirmation that even their parents consider them to be failures or freaks. No victim ever went to school or to a playground with the intent of getting picked on. As a parent, you need to understand that if it were so easy to just "toughen up," bullying would not happen in the first place.

Identify characteristics or behaviors that may make your child susceptible to bullying.

Victims who are bullied for reasons that they have some control over must be willing to help themselves. This is not about blaming them. Rather, it is about empowerment. Victims need to know if they are contributing to their own victimization. And if they are, they must learn what they can do differently so that they are not such tempting targets. This doesn't mean every child must be turned into a machine that looks, acts, and sounds alike. Remember the story of Andre in Chapter 2? He was the junior high student who preferred to play with action figures and read at recess rather than join his classmates in more "conventional" activities like football and basketball. Andre's interests did not conform to what his peers deemed "normal," and he paid a price. The uniqueness of children like Andre is ideal and should be celebrated. But sometimes children need to be selective about where, when, and how they showcase their unconventional selves.

If you have a child who has interests that fall outside the range of what a majority of kids are interested in, that's okay. The key is finding friendlier environments where those interests will be appreciated. For Andre, he just wanted the teasing to stop. His parents and teachers helped him see that he had other options available. He decided to participate in team games during recess. But he didn't give up his action figures. He just left them at home. That way he could indulge his interests far away from the sneers and jeers of his peers. Some parents find this strategy difficult, especially if they feel their child isn't doing anything wrong. They demand that everyone else change their attitudes and behaviors instead. In situations like these, parents have to remember the ultimate objective. For Andre and other victims, they just want the teasing and abuse to stop.

Making Better Choices

Andre's story is interesting because it highlights the powerful role problem-solving skills play in helping children break the

FINDING A SENSE OF STRENGTH

"Every time I walked out the door, with a bow in my hair and hopeful look on my face, the neighborhood kids would torment me, pushing me, knocking me down and teasing me until I burst into tears and ran back in the house, where I would stay for the rest of the day. ...After this had gone on for several weeks, my mother met me one day as I ran in the door. She took me by the shoulders, told me there was no room for cowards in our house and sent me back outside. I was shocked, and so were the neighborhood kids, who had not expected to see me so soon.

When they challenged me again, I stood up for myself and finally won some friends...

As my mother taught me, even very young children can be given a sense of strength in the face of indifference or cruelty."

– SENATOR HILLARY RODHAM CLINTON
From *It Takes a Village*

cycle of bullying. Andre's teachers and parents helped him look at the problem, see the realities of the situation, think of potential options, and decide on a course of action that would produce the desired outcome. By doing all of that, he made a thoughtful, successful decision. Kids who avoid trouble or are able to work through difficult situations know how to make good decisions. As a parent, you can help your children make better choices by teaching them **SODAS**.

SODAS is an acronym that stands for **S**ituation, **O**ptions, **D**isadvantages, **A**dvantages, and **S**olution. Regardless of the role your child plays in a bullying situation – bully, victim, or bystander – this decision-making method can help him or her see the real issues and begin to find more acceptable solutions so the problem will not continue. Here is how each step works:

Define the SITUATION – In this stage, your child identifies the who, what, where, when, and why questions so that you have a complete and accurate picture of what actually went down. You can help this process along by asking your child open-ended questions that encourage him or her to provide as much information as possible. For example, if your child was acting aggressively, you want to know the circumstances surrounding the incident. Did someone make your child mad? Was your child just joking around? Does he or she simply not like someone?

List the OPTIONS – These are the choices your child has. Most problems or decisions have several options. Help your child think of as many options as possible. Too often, a child sees every decision as an "all or nothing" proposition. For example, a bully picks on another child so the victim's only solution is to fight the bully. Your role as a parent is to get your child to open his or her mind to other possibilities. Here are tips for helping your child identify options:

- Have your child list his or her options. Be careful not to make any decisions right away as to whether those options are "good" or "bad." The purpose here is to help your child learn to make decisions on his or her own.

- Try to keep the number of options to three or four. Any more than that can be confusing. Also try to make sure that at least one option is reasonable and has a good chance of success.

- Suggest options if your child struggles to come up with some.

Think of the DISADVANTAGES/ADVANTAGES – In this step, talk to your child about the pros and cons of each option. This helps your child see the connection between each option and what could happen if that option is chosen. Ask your child what's good and bad about each option, including why each may or may not work.

Choose a SOLUTION – The final step in the SODAS process is choosing the option that your child thinks will get the best result. It is possible your child will choose a solution you disagree with. If your child's decision won't hurt anyone else, is not illegal, and does not contradict your moral beliefs, then let it stand. He or she will learn from the decision, and if the outcome isn't what the child hoped for, another option can be tried.

A similar, though slightly abbreviated, version of SODAS is **POP,** which stands for **P**roblem, **O**ptions, and **P**lan. Again, this decision-making method helps children, especially younger ones, clarify what the problem is, identify the options they have for dealing with it, and then actually follow through on their decision. When you sit down and go through this process, you do more than just strengthen your child's ability to make better judgments. You strengthen your relationship with him or her. You want your child to share with you so that you know what's going on in his or her life. The parent who is available and involved is much more likely to calm a belligerent bully, give backbone to a bystander, and teach a victim to overcome fear and confront problems assertively.

---

[1] Parents of bullying victims, as quoted in Marc Hansen, "Bullying of kids isn't just one town's problem," *Des Moines Register,* June 8, 2004.

chapter 11

By **Kathleen McGee, M.A.**

Preventing Sexualized Bullying

All of the techniques and skills described in previous chapters to help bullies and victims can be applied to situations of sexual bullying. Remember that aggression is inappropriate regardless of whether there is a sexual component. The key is to always focus on the behavior.

This chapter offers advice for parents on how to educate children about the sexual messages and attitudes that dominate today's pop culture, including what moms and dads can do to help their children respect themselves and the personal boundaries of others. But before we get to the role of parents, let's look at what can be done to keep kids safe when they're away from home. Here are three recommendations for schools, youth clubs, and other social organizations to follow if they want to minimize the threat of sexual bullies.

What Schools, Organizations Can Do

Develop a "zero-tolerance" policy on sexual harassment.

An effective policy will specifically name the behaviors that are prohibited. The sexually suggestive behaviors highlighted in Chapter 4 provide a good starting point. A good policy will also include a range of potential consequences for anyone engaging in inappropriate sexual behavior. Consequences can range from verbal warnings (for the first minor offense) or teacher-student conferences (after repeated offenses) to suspensions or expulsions after major, repeated infractions. The policy should also identify the people who need to be made aware of a child's violation of the policy. For example, a first-time minor offense like using vulgar language may not warrant informing an administrator or parent. But repeated offenses or serious acts of aggression, such as spreading obscene material or groping someone, would involve an administrator, parent or caretaker, counselor, and possibly the police.

A National Institute of Child Health and Human Development survey of more than 15,000 students found that girls were more likely to be bullied about their looks through sexual comments and rumors than boys.

Journal of the American Medical Association, 2001

Every situation has its own unique set of circumstances, so the policy should give administrators some degree of discretion. Ideally, consequences will be based on the frequency and severity of the behavior. Zero tolerance does not mean that any infraction results in a child getting kicked out of a school or program. It merely means that penalties will be imposed on anyone who violates the sexual harassment policy. In addition, children, staff, volunteers, and parents need to be informed of the policy and how it will be enforced. In school situations, we recommend that officials go over the policy with students, staff, and parents at least once each semester.

Provide training for staff, parents, and volunteers.

The training should include a clear and concise definition of sexual harassment or bullying, including legal responsibilities and youth rights. Training should also cover what sexual bullying looks and sounds like, how to respond to and correct the behavior when it happens, and what consequences are appropriate. The reason we recommend training is because of the consistency it provides. Training puts everyone on the same page in terms of how to deal with the behaviors. As a result, children hear a clear and consistent message that sexually aggressive behavior will not be tolerated.

Teach children how to identify and report sexual harassment.

Let kids know, specifically, the types of inappropriate behavior and language that are unacceptable and what the consequences will be for anyone who chooses to engage in such behaviors. Here is a list of behaviors that you may want to discuss with them:

Verbal, nonverbal, or written

- Putdowns, insults, name-calling (slut, bitch, fag), swearing, sexual gossip, catcalls

Physical

- Hitting, punching, pinching, biting, arm twisting, shoving, choking, grabbing, slapping, kicking

- Intimidating gestures (making a fist, pointing to or at private body parts), blocking exits, punching walls, knocking things around

- Restraining or pinning someone against a wall or door, or blocking their movements

- Sexual gestures, stares, whistling, stalking

After you have identified the behaviors, you need to explain how to go about reporting incidents of sexual bullying or harassment. Understand that this can be very difficult for some youth. Kids are reluctant to come forward if they believe the bullies will retaliate, or they think adults will only make the problem worse. Whatever reporting mechanisms you have available, make sure they protect those doing the reporting. In a way, you need a version of the witness protection program. Without it, kids will never step forward, especially if they see those who did get ostracized by their peers or embarrassed by adults.

One of the best ways for kids to report abuse is to tell someone they trust, such as a parent, teacher, counselor, or pastor. In order for kids to have the confidence and ability to approach someone and report sexual harassment, they need to know what to do. Here are the steps you can teach kids on how to go about reporting sexual harassment:

1. Stay calm.
2. Gain an adult's attention appropriately.
3. Say, "Could I speak to you alone?"
4. Describe the incident.
5. Answer all questions factually, and make only truthful statements.
6. Say, "Thank you for listening."

When a child comes to you and says he or she is being bullied in a sexual way, you also need to remain calm. Your first instinct may be to charge off and confront the alleged perpetrator. Instead, gather as much information as you possibly can. Ask open-ended questions so you can figure out what happened. Find out who was involved, and where and when the incident(s) occurred. Assure the child that you can be trusted, and that you will help him or her deal with the problem. Thank the child for being open with you. Don't be afraid to ask what, if any, role the "victim" may have played in the situation. It's entirely possible the child may have initiated the trouble by making inappropriate jokes or comments, but then didn't appreciate or anticipate the type of reaction he or she generated. Understanding exactly what happened and the reasons why will help you avoid punishing the innocent and protecting the guilty. Your objective should always be to work toward problem resolution, not problem escalation.

Parents as Protectors

While policies in schools or other places where your child spends time are necessary and can be effective deterrents to sexual bullying and harassment, they cannot replace the influence you have as a parent to shape your child's behavior. One of the most effective things you can do to help your children avoid victimization is to teach them about personal boundaries. You should already be familiar with this concept. Boundaries are the limits you set for relationships. They help you to recognize what is and what is not your responsibility, and define what is acceptable or unacceptable in relationships.

All children need to know how to establish appropriate physical, emotional, and sexual boundaries. They must also learn to respect others' personal "space." If they don't, they are at much greater risk for becoming a sexual bully or becoming a victim of one. It's never too late to teach children about establishing and respecting boundaries. Here are some things you can teach your children to do to develop positive relationships and healthy boundaries:

Identify trustworthy peers and make friends with them.

Trustworthiness is an abstract concept, and simply telling your child to look for trustworthy peers may not be much help. You need to teach your children what it means to be trustworthy, and how to see it in others. Explain how trustworthy individuals possess and repeatedly demonstrate four special characteristics: integrity (the courage to resist temptation); honesty (the ability to be sincere and be truthful); reliability (the willingness to honor commitments); and loyalty (the strength to stand with someone in need).

Children who possess these qualities are more likely to develop friendships, which is one of the best defenses against a bully's unwanted attention. And kids who have values such as honesty, sincerity, and integrity are less likely to bully others, sexually or otherwise.

Trust your feelings of comfort or discomfort.

Feelings are good indicators of right and wrong. Let your children know that if someone makes them feel uncomfortable or threatened, they should share their concerns with you or someone else they trust. Also explain that it's not okay for them to engage in behaviors that intimidate others. This is a good time to remind your kids of the Golden Rule. They should treat others the same way they want to be treated. So if they don't want to be insulted, ignored, or intimidated, they shouldn't behave that way toward others.

Speak up when someone or something bothers you.

Assertiveness is a skill all children need but one that bullies and victims lack. An assertive person communicates his or her needs **and** still shows respect and concern for the needs of others. The best way for your children to learn this skill is to practice it. First, they should try to be more assertive with you and other family members. By learning how to express themselves positively toward the people closest to them, they will have the confidence and the ability to be more assertive in other relationships and situations. If your children are passive, have them practice making "I" statements. For example, if they have an opinion or want to express their feelings, they can assert themselves with comments, such as "I think ..." or " I wish...."

These general rules can help your children establish and maintain healthy boundaries in all of their relationships. More importantly, it makes them less vulnerable to the manipulation and language cons of sexual bullies. Teaching your children how to be assertive and follow the Golden Rule has other benefits as well. You provide them with an understanding of what it means to have and to show respect. You also reinforce positive values that are sometimes lacking in the world our kids inhabit.

Parents as Media Filters

The more our kids are exposed to negative words and images, the more likely they are to think such things are okay. Your job is to help them see through the manipulative, distorted, and harmful messages they pick up from television, movies, music, and videos. Here are a few strategies to help you do that:

Be a positive influence.

If you watch sexually explicit programs, laugh at sexually degrading jokes and comments, or use profane language, your 9- or 10-year-old may think that it's okay to do the same. Take a look at the messages you allow into your home. You can block some of the media's intrusion by occasionally turning off the TV.

Spend an evening reading books, playing games, or volunteering in the community. Monitor what programs your children are tuning into and be selective about what you allow them to watch, read, or listen to.

If you have a habit of making off-color remarks to describe people or situations, be aware that your kids are listening. When

SEX AND VIOLENCE VIA THE INTERNET

Young people's exposure to aggressive sexual solicitation and unwanted sexual material via the Internet occurs with surprising frequency. A national study of youth (between the ages of 10 and 17) who are regular Internet users revealed:

- 25% experienced unwanted exposure to people engaged in sex acts or pictures of naked people in the last year.

- One in 17 was threatened or harassed.

- Roughly 25% of kids exposed to unwanted sexual content or who were harassed were upset by the experience.

- Approximately 25% of youth who received a sexual solicitation told a parent.

- Just 17% of youth (and 10% of parents) could identify a specific authority (Internet service provider, FBI, or CyberTipline) to whom they could report their experiences.

From Online Victimization: A Report on the Nation's Youth *survey by the National Center for Missing & Exploited Children, (2000)* you use profanity or say something derogatory in front of your children, apologize. Showing regret and explaining why your remarks are hurtful can be a powerful teaching moment – one your kids won't soon forget. Remember that the main thing is to set a positive example.

Teach your kids to be media literate.

Many children and teens don't even think about what they're tuning into. They're just occupying their time. You can teach them how to judge whether messages are junk, truthful, or inaccurate by talking to them about the content. For example, talk about the relationships that are depicted between males and females. Do they reflect how things should be, or how things really are? What's good and what's bad about the relationships? Is someone being victimized or taken advantage of? If so, how? By asking questions and making your children think about the messages they're receiving, you help to develop their critical-thinking skills, and they become more than passive observers.

Provide positive alternatives.

Media have the most influence when other influences are absent. Don't make the celebrity culture the center of your family's entertainment life. The more time your children spend in activities that broaden their minds (reading, arts and crafts) and strengthen their bodies (sports and exercise), the less time they have to spend staring at a TV, computer, or PlayStation videogame. Other ways you can maximize the benefits and minimize the problems of media include:

- Set limits on the amount of time your kids watch TV, surf the Web, or play videogames.

- Remember that computers can drain the brain, too.

- Evaluate what your kids are watching, listening to, or logging on to.

- Encourage your children to choose quality programs.

- Watch TV or movies with your kids, monitor the videogames they want to play, and listen to their CDs and tapes.

Following through on these suggestions is one way you can keep your children from becoming desensitized to today's sex-saturated culture. While it's impossible to protect your kids from every harmful message, you can instill in your children values and skills that will make them less susceptible to believing – and practicing – the warped attitudes and behaviors that are being sold as "normal."

By **Laura Buddenberg**

Safety in Cyberspace

A big bullying battleground is cyberspace. Young people are misusing the Internet and programs like instant messaging to harass, humiliate, and manipulate their enemies and their friends. How unsettled were you when reading the IM conversation between Katie and Elizabeth in Chapter 5? The suicide threat by Katie, the seeming indifference by Elizabeth. Maybe it was all innocent fun, but maybe it wasn't. How do you know?

In the world of online chat, interpreting another's intentions is not always simple. As parents, we don't want our kids to be manipulated, yet we sometimes fail to show them how to avoid trouble. You might tell your daughter not to talk to strangers on the street, but do you tell her not to talk to strangers on the Internet? You might tell your son never to say vulgar four-letter words, but do you tell him he shouldn't type those words when chatting online? You might warn your kids not to act like bullies at school, but do you tell them what your behavior expectations are in other situations, like cyberspace?

What Parents Can Do

How do you protect children in a boundary-free environment where deception is easy, privacy is an illusion, and anonymity is an excuse to be uninhibited? For starters, you set boundaries for online behavior. You provide consequences when boundaries are broken. And, you structure how technology like instant messaging and the Internet are used. Here are ways this can be done in your home:

Know the Technology

Software programs and capabilities are constantly changing, and it can seem overwhelming when you're exhausted by the daily grind of work and family. The good news is that you don't have to become an expert on every computer program or innovation to be effective. You do, however, need an awareness of what your kids are using and doing online.

Part of being aware means understanding that your kids, especially if they are computer whizzes, might disguise their online activities. Sophisticated users can employ stealthy tactics. For example, they might rename the instant messaging software that they downloaded off the Internet – without your permission – so you don't realize you actually have it. Or, if they don't want you to know they visited a forbidden Web site, they might erase the Web browser's history.

If you don't think you're as sophisticated about computers as your kids, you may be able to find the help you need at your children's school. Many have technology specialists who are attuned to what kids do online. Talk to them to find out what you should know. Maybe they will be willing to conduct a mini-workshop and introduce parents to the programs their kids are using. They could also talk about the opportunities and obstacles that certain software programs pose. If your school doesn't have a technology specialist, perhaps there is a parent or professional in the community who has expertise in this area. He or she might be willing to talk about how programs like instant messaging can be used and controlled.

Monitor Computer Use

Try to keep home computers in common areas like family rooms or dens, not in your children's bedrooms. Proximity makes observation easier and more effective. Know your kids' usernames and passwords. You should also invest in monitoring software. Several affordable options exist (for more information, visit www.getnetwise.org), including programs that allow you to track and print out instant messages word for word. Let your kids know that you are watching their online activity. Don't let cries of "right to privacy" intimidate you into backing off. If you thought your son was smoking pot in his bedroom, would you stand outside the door and wish he would stop? In your house, you have a duty to protect your children. They need to know that instant messaging and the Internet are conveniences, not necessities, and they can be taken away if misused.

When children know you check the Web sites they visit and read their IM conversations, they are much less likely to put themselves in bad situations. Making your kids aware that they are being monitored also provides them an easy out if someone starts using profanity, spreading rumors, or gossiping. Your children can easily type, "My mom will be reading this later. Let's talk about something else." That may be enough, especially for their friends, to stop them from going any further. When that doesn't work, your children should remove themselves from the situation by logging off.

Some experts suggest that young children should literally pull the plug on the computer if they get messages that make them uncomfortable or scared. Their reasoning is that it's faster and easier than going through all the steps of shutting down the program. Others counter that recommendation by arguing that repeatedly pulling the plug could damage the computer. They suggest young kids have a bell or whistle with them to get someone's attention. We believe that young kids should never be left alone at the computer in the first place. If they're too young to boot up a program or logoff the computer properly, then they're not ready to go solo on the Web.

You can also make it easier on yourself by limiting the amount of time children spend online. Restrictions should be based on the age and maturity of each child, as well as his or her purpose for being online. For example, a junior in high school should be given more latitude when doing a research assignment than a sibling who just wants to surf the Net for fun. To monitor instant messaging, you may want to have a rule that it cannot be used when a parent or other responsible adult is not present.

There will be moments, maybe many, when you're simply too busy or tired to look over the logs of every IM conversation. That will happen. You can't catch everything, maybe not a lot of things. But periodic monitoring can provide you with valuable insights into your children's lives, including the boundaries they have in their relationships. When you see things that trouble you (a sure sign that you should increase your monitoring), ask your children to explain the situation. Let them talk before you make accusations or insert your opinions. An open discussion with your children will provide more information than the words you read on a printout.

Teach Online Etiquette

You wouldn't hand your teenager the keys to a new car and then walk away without saying a word. You would introduce him or her to its features and explain the rules of the road. Similarly, your kids need to know the proper way to navigate the Internet. Here are four laws that you might want to enforce:

- No profanity, threats, mean comments, or inappropriately personal questions and conversations (initiated by them or others). Remind your kids that if they would be too embarrassed or ashamed to say something in front of their grandparents, then they shouldn't say it to anyone online. They should assume that someone's mother will eventually see their messages.

- Do not give out your name, parent's name, address, phone number, passwords, credit card numbers, and other personal information about yourself or the family.

- If you receive harassing messages or are the subject of rumors, tell Mom or Dad immediately. Show your kids how to block ugly messages coming from unknown or undesirable sources. Make it clear, however, that they shouldn't block messages as a way of "virtually" excluding friends or classmates.

- Be honest. If others are with you, let the people you're chatting with know you are not alone, and tell them who else is in the room. If you step away from the computer, don't let anyone take your place and pretend to be you.

These laws will be easier to remember and enforce if you write them down. Creating an Internet contract that both you and your children sign is a great way to clarify expectations.

(See pages 188-190 for a sample contract you can use with your children.) Everyone will know exactly what the rules are, so arbitrarily ignoring some rules, forgetting others, or claiming "ignorance" won't work. The contract also serves as a visual reminder of everyone's obligations. Most kids don't want to disappoint their parents. When they sign their names on the dotted line, they will be motivated to live up to their end of the bargain. And like any other contract, they should be held accountable if they violate any of the rules.

Use Consequences

As you know, kids love to test boundaries. So what do you do when they violate one of the laws you have for Internet use? You need to provide a negative consequence. For a major infraction, such as using profanity or spreading malicious rumors, take instant messaging away from them for a week or more. Have them apologize to anyone they hurt. Likewise, if your child fails to stop someone from using profanity or gossiping online, there should be negative consequences for remaining silent. You can block your child from corresponding with that individual or take IM away for a few days. When imposing a consequence, it should be based on the severity and frequency of the problem.

Taking away something your children enjoy is a powerful motivator for them to change their behavior. But consequences should never be limited to the negative. You need to applaud the positive things your children do online. If you see that they stood up to someone who was becoming mean or if they consistently follow your rules, praise them. Tell them they're doing a good job. You might extend their IM privileges by 15 extra minutes a week or reward them with something else they like doing. Positive consequences are great behavior enforcers!

Check Buddy Lists

Some instant messaging programs have space for up to 200 names on a buddy list. Even for the socially connected, that's excessive. Ask your kids to identify the people behind every screen name. If they don't know who someone is, delete the name from their list. If they tell you it belongs to a friend of a friend whom they have never met, remove the name. Instant messaging is like inviting people into your home. You should at least know who you're asking inside.

Take Threats Seriously

Make sure your kids know that they should tell you **immediately** if anyone online, "friend" or not, threatens to hurt others or commit suicide. If you are not home when the threat is made, your kids need to stop the online conversation right away, turn off the computer, and contact you. If they can't reach you, have a back-up number for them to call, such as the Boys Town National Hotline at 1-800-448-3000.

Final Words

Technology is only as good as the people who use it. Your first instinct may be to remove your children completely from instant messaging and the whole online experience. But that would be like throwing the baby out with the bathwater. You don't want to inadvertently keep your children out of the social loop or be unnecessarily isolated when they don't have to be. If you monitor your children's activities, give them boundaries, and teach them how to act responsibly, they can have a rich and rewarding experience. Better still, if you show them how to stand up to cyberbullies, they may gain the confidence to use those skills in other situations and environments.

It's important to note that any time your children are online, they potentially could have a real-time chat with a friend or stranger, even if it's not through instant messaging. All sorts of interactive Web sites can host live chat rooms. For example, popular game sites have chat rooms and discussion boards where players can talk in real time about their passions for the game, among other things. The more responsible sites have moderators to monitor comments and block anyone who becomes vulgar or inappropriate. But that's not true at every site. Kids need to be reminded not to share personal information. And they will need to be reminded again and again.

How do you protect children in a boundary-free environment where deception is easy, privacy is an illusion, and anonymity is an excuse to be uninhibited?

Teaching Internet safety and online etiquette cannot be a one-and-done moment. Constant monitoring and teaching are required.

Another popular device that has become an unexpected weapon in the hands of bullies is the cell phone. Bullies use them to text-message threats to their victims. Now cell phones are also cameras. Bullies and others are using cell phones to take secret snapshots of people in compromising positions. Often, the photos end up on the Web. School locker rooms are an area where picture phones have been used to capture people in various stages of undress. The problem has gotten so bad, Congress passed legislation making "video voyeurism" a crime punishable by fine, imprisonment, or both.

When you set up cell phone plans for your children, remember to focus on what is needed rather than what is wanted. If the primary reason for giving your kids a cell phone is for safety and convenience, then features like text messaging and pictures are not necessary. If the phone is to be used only for emergencies, then don't sign up for an unlimited calling plan. You can create limits for your children that they may not be willing to set for themselves.

All of this new technology may seem overwhelming or intimidating at times, but nobody loves your children or has more invested in their success than you. The suggestions we've provided in this chapter and throughout the book will go a long way in keeping your children safe no matter what environment they're in.

THE SAFE INTERNET-
SURFING CONTRACT

My Agreement About Using the Internet

I want to use the Internet. I know that there are certain rules about what I should do online. I agree to follow these rules and my parents agree to help me follow these rules:

1. I will not give my name, address, telephone number, school, or my parents' names, addresses, or telephone numbers, or anything else that would help anyone find me offline (like the name of my sports team) to anyone I meet on the computer.

2. I understand that some people online pretend to be someone else. Sometimes they pretend to be kids, when they're really grown-ups. I will tell my parents about people I meet online. I will also tell my parents before I answer any e-mails or instant messages I receive from – or send e-mail or instant messages to – new people I meet online.

3. I will not buy or order anything online or give out any credit card information without asking my parents.

4. I will not fill out any form online that asks me for any information about myself or my family without first getting permission from my parents. This includes forms for contests or registering at a site. I'll also check to see if the sites have a privacy policy, and if they promise to keep my private information private. If they don't promise to keep my private information private, I won't give them any private information. (I will talk to my parents about what "private information" is.)

5. I will not get into arguments or fights online. If someone tries to start an argument or fight with me, I won't answer him or her and will tell my parents.

6. If I see something I do not like, or that makes me uncomfortable, or that I know my parents don't want me to see, I will click on the "Back" button or log off.

7. If I see people doing things or saying things to other kids online I know they're not supposed to do or say, I'll tell my parents.

8. I won't keep online secrets from my parents.

9. If someone sends me any pictures, links to sites I know I shouldn't be going to, or any e-mail or instant messages that use bad language, I will tell my parents.

10. If someone asks me to do something I am not supposed to do, I will tell my parents.

11. I will not call anyone I met online unless my parents say it's okay. (Even then I will block caller ID by pressing *57 on my phone.)

12. I will never meet "in person" anyone I met online, unless my parents say it's okay and they are with me.

13. I will never send anything to anyone I meet online, unless my parents say it's okay.

14. If anyone I meet online sends me anything, I will tell my parents.

15. I will not use something I found online and pretend it's mine.

16. I won't say bad things about people online, and I will practice good Netiquette.

17. I won't use bad language online or threaten anyone, even if I'm only kidding.

18. I know that my parents want to make sure I'm safe online, and I will listen to them when they ask me not to do something.

19. I will help teach my parents more about computers and the Internet.

20. I will practice safe computing, and check for viruses whenever I borrow a disk from someone or download something, or open any attachment, even from someone I know.

21. I will tell my parents when something bad happens online, because they promise not to overreact. And I will remember that it's not my fault if others do bad things online!

I promise to follow these rules.
(signed by child/teen)

I promise to help my child follow these rules and not to overreact if my child tells me about bad things that happen in cyberspace.
(signed by parent)

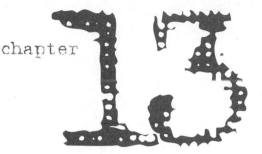

By **José Bolton, Sr., Ph.D., L.P.C.,**
Stan Graeve, M.A

Final Thoughts

This is our call to action. Bullying is alive and well in environments where our children gather and where adults are absent (literally and figuratively), whether it's in our schools, on our neighborhood playgrounds, or in Internet chat rooms. Our hope is that you come to understand, just as the group of New England educators did in our introduction, that bullying should never be considered an inevitable, inescapable, or acceptable rite of passage. Yes, kids will be teased or sometimes feel threatened, but that is not the same as the relentless intimidation that defines bullying. We do not serve our children well if we continue to dismiss this behavior as simply "kids being kids."

Bullying is a systemic problem that requires systemic solutions. In other words, victims cannot be expected to make bullies less abusive or bystanders more understanding all by themselves. A classroom teacher who has little support from school administrators cannot be expected to improve a school's entire social climate. Everyone involved in a child's life has a role in shaping and influencing his or her behavior. But changing behavior is made more difficult if you ignore that behavior's relationship to its environment. To paraphrase Father Flanagan, there is no such thing as a bad child; there is only bad example, bad thinking, bad training, and bad environment.

Bullying behavior is a difficult problem to address. Hopefully, the strategies and ideas presented here will give you new insights and more hope for dealing with this issue in your families, schools, and communities. We realize that this book does not represent the final word on the subject. What we have tried to offer you is a fresh perspective and a new way of thinking about how the environment affects behavior and vice versa. The action plans we've presented are really jumping-off points. Some strategies may not complement your specific situation, but you can certainly modify them or incorporate elements into what you're already doing. The most important thing to remember is that ignoring bullies and pretending they are someone else's responsibility only exacerbates the problem and its harmful effects.

Our children have a fundamental right to not only feel safe, but to actually be safe. As parents, educators, and people who work with and care about children, we must commit ourselves to ensuring that no child is subjected to constant fear, humiliation, or persecution. Rather, we must focus our attention on making a difference that matters to children: teaching respect, stopping abuse, and rewarding kindness.

part iii

For More Information

Helpful Resources

There are many nonprofit organizations, governmental agencies, and advocacy groups dedicated to fostering healthier social environments for children. The resources listed in this section provide information on many of the issues – health, safety, school and community partnerships, prevention, and parenting – that affect, and are affected by, bullying. Listing these organizations in this section does not imply that the authors agree with or endorse all of their material or conclusions.

Boys Town National Hotline
1-800-448-3000

Staffed by professional counselors, 24 hours a day, 7 days a week, this hotline is available for children and parents with questions or problems of any kind, including bullying, violence, suicide, and relationships. Referrals to local services and resources can be made.

Your Life, Your Voice
www.yourlifeyourvoice.org

Your Life, Your Voice is an interactive Web site operated by the Boys Town National Hotline that enables and encourages teens to share their problems, concerns, and challenges in positive, creative ways. Teens can submit artwork, photos, poetry, and other means of self-expression to illustrate their thoughts and feelings. They also can ask questions and get answers from trained counselors to the challenges they may be facing.

www.parenting.org

Moms, dads, and caregivers will find sound advice on rearing children at this site. Articles written by Boys Town parenting experts tackle issues ranging from separation anxiety to stealing and cheating. There are several articles on bullying and aggression. Content is appropriate for parents of children of all ages, from toddlers to teens. A free parenting e-booklet, available in English and Spanish, also can be downloaded.

PBS Kids

www.pbskids.org/itsmylife/friends

This interactive Web site includes games, video clips, kids' opinion polls, and quotes from some of today's most popular young celebrities talking about their own challenges growing up. The site also has a message board where kids can share their experiences and thoughts on handling bullying problems. Articles and lesson plans for parents and teachers are also provided.

Stop Bullying Now!

The U.S. Department of Health and Human Services
200 Independence Ave., S.W.
Washington, D.C. 20201
1-877-696-6775 (toll-free)
www.stopbullyingnow.hrsa.gov/kids

The Web site offers something for children, parents, and educators. The "What Kids Can Do" page features animated "webisodes," games, and expert advice to help young people, whether they are bullies, bullied, or bystanders. The "What Adults Can Do" page has helpful classroom materials for teachers and tips to guide parents whose children are dealing with bullying.

Fight Crime: Invest in Kids

1212 New York Ave., NW, Suite 300
Washington, D.C. 20005
www.fightcrime.org

This nonprofit coalition of law enforcement officials, prosecutors, and victims of violence advocates for increased funding for early childhood programs and anti-bullying programs. Opinion polls, research reports, and updates on legislative issues can be found on its Web site.

Bullying.org Canada

www.bullying.org

Visitors to this online site have access to information on bullying issues as well as support services. There are two moderated online support groups, one for youth and one for adults, that users can subscribe to. Young people are encouraged to share their feelings by submitting personal stories, poems, and bullying-related skits or lyrics. The site includes a bullying survey and an anti-bullying pledge.

www.stopbullying.org

This site features an animated bullying story written by young students from the United Kingdom. Visitors can help propel the story along by making decisions or choices for the character. Each choice leads to a different outcome. Free sample lesson plans and interactive activities, based on the animated story, allow teachers and students to explore the issue of bullying.

Easing the Teasing

www.easingtheteasing.com

Created by Judy S. Freedman, a licensed clinical social worker and author, the content addresses the problem of teasing and how it can lead to verbal bullying. Visitors can download a free "What is Teasing?" survey, which can be reproduced for classroom use. A list of 10 strategies to help kids deal with teasing is also offered in a printable format.

National PTA

541 N. Fairbanks Court, Suite 1300
Chicago, IL 60611
1-800-307-4PTA (4782)
www.pta.org

PTA is the largest volunteer child advocacy organization in the United States and offers resources and advice to help parents, educators, and others get involved in creating healthier social environments for children in schools and communities. The Web site has tips for helping children deal with bullies and sexual harassment and tips for protecting young people from gangs and violence.

MedlinePlus

U.S. National Library of Medicine
8600 Rockville Pike
Bethesda, MD 20894
www.nlm.nih.gov/medlineplus/bullying.html

Updated daily, this online health information service offers articles, research reports, and other resources on a broad spectrum of health issues, including the effects of bullying. There are numerous links to articles that discuss bullying topics, from prevention and coping strategies to factors associated with bullying behaviors and victimization. The site is maintained by the National Institutes of Health.

Education World

www.educationworld.com

This is a complete online resource for educators that includes topical stories, education-related news, lesson plans, and research materials. The site has posted several articles related to bullying and its effects on classrooms and schools.

National Mental Health Information Center

United States Department of Health and Human Services –
Substance Abuse and Mental Health Services Administration
P.O. Box 42557
Washington, D.C. 20015
1-800-789-2647
1-866-889-2647 (TDD)
www.mentalhealth.samhsa.gov

Parents, educators, and other caregivers can use the Web site to learn more about the mental health challenges that young people, including bullies, victims, and bystanders, struggle with. The site posts articles on bullying, school violence, and suicide prevention. There is also information on the Safe Schools/Healthy Students Initiative and other federal grant programs.

GetNetWise

Internet Education Foundation
1634 I St., N.W., Suite 1100
Washington, D.C. 20006
www.getnetwise.org

This public service Web site is designed to help Internet users have a safe, enjoyable, and educational experience online. Important information, including links to Internet safety products that block explicit or violent content, is available. Parents will appreciate the advice, resources, and strategies offered to protect families from online victimization.

Center for Safe and Responsible Internet Use

474 W. 29th Ave.
Eugene, OR 97405
541-556-1145
www.cyberbully.org

This organization promotes the safe and responsible use of the Internet. The Web site provides educators, parents, and others with resources, including an educators' guide and parents' guide to cyberbullying, that offer advice on how to prevent and detect online harassment.

i-Safe America, Inc.

5900 Pasteur Court
Suite #100
Carlsbad, CA 92008
760-603-7911
www.isafe.org

This nonprofit Internet safety foundation provides age-appropriate curriculums (K-12) to schools. It also has cybersafety programs for educators, parents, law enforcement officers, and community leaders.

The Children's Partnership (TCP)

2000 P Street, NW, Suite 330
Washington, D.C. 20036
202-429-0033
www.childrenspartnership.org

This site offers downloadable material – A Parent's Guide to Online Kids and The Parent's Guide to the Information Superhighway – that answers many of the questions and concerns parents have about Internet safety and their children's online activities.

National Association for Media Literacy Education

10 Laurel Hill Drive
Cheery Hill, NJ 08003
1-888-775-2652
www.amlainfo.org

This national membership organization sponsors advocacy programs and activities to increase media literacy for children, parents, and educators.

Bam! Body and Mind

Centers for Disease Control and Prevention
1600 Clifton Road
MS C-04
Atlanta, Georgia 30333
800-311-3435
www.bam.gov/sub_yourlife/index.htm

BAM! is a child-friendly Web site (ideal for kids ages 9 to 13) with advice on making healthy life choices. Young people will have fun playing interactive online games, including "The Bully Roundup," which tests their bully smarts, and "Grind Your Mind," an animated quiz on peer pressure.

National Center for Injury Prevention and Control

4770 Buford Highway NE
MS F-63
Atlanta, GA 30341-3724
800-232-4636
www.cdc.gov/injury/publications/index.html

The Centers for Disease Control's Injury Center offers a number of free publications in a variety of formats, including hard copy, online viewing, and downloadable documents from its Web site. The publications cover a range of health issues, from youth suicide prevention programs to activity guides on preventing youth violence.

McGruff the Crime Dog®

National Crime Prevention Council
2345 Crystal Drive, Suite 500
Arlington, VA 22202
www.mcgruff.org

Educators, parents and kids can visit McGruff's Web site to learn about bullying, including cyberbullies. Free downloadable resources, in English and Spanish, offer advice on how to help children who are bullies or victims. Young visitors can read comic stories about bullying and play online games.

Recommended Reading

Beane, Allan. *The Bully-Free Classroom.* Minneapolis, MN: Free Spirit (1999).

Borba, Michele. *Parents Do Make a Difference.* San Francisco: Jossey-Bass (1999).

Burke, Ray and Herron, Ron. *Common Sense Parenting.* Boys Town, NE: Boys Town Press (1996).

Coloroso, Barbara. *The Bully, the Bullied, and the Bystander.* New York: HarperCollins (2003).

Dahlberg, Linda and Toal, Susan and Behrens, Christopher. *Measuring Violence-Related Attitudes, Beliefs, and Behaviors Among Youths: A Compendium of Assessment Tools.* Atlanta, GA: Centers for Disease Control and Prevention, National Center for Injury Prevention and Control (1998). Available for free online at: http://www.cdc.gov/ncipc/pub-res/measure.htm

Dellasega, Cheryl and Nixon, Charisse. *Girl Wars.* New York: Fireside (2003).

Evans, Patricia. *Teen Torment.* Avon, MA: Adams Media (2003).

Freedman, Judy S. *Easing the Teasing.* Chicago: Contemporary Books (2002).

Garbarino, James and DeLara, Ellen. *And Words Can Hurt Forever.* New York: Free Press (2002).

Hyland, Terry and Davis, Jerry. *Angry Kids, Frustrated Parents.* Boys Town, NE: Boys Town Press (1999).

Kaufman, Gershen and Raphael, Lev and Espeland, Pamela. *A Teacher's Guide to Stick Up for Yourself!* Minneapolis, MN: Free Spirit (2000).

McGee, Kathleen and Buddenberg, Laura. *Unmasking Sexual Con Games: Leader's Guide.* Boys Town, NE: Boys Town Press (2003).

McGee, Kathleen and Buddenberg, Laura. *Unmasking Sexual Con Games: Teen's Guide.* Boys Town, NE: Boys Town Press (2003).

Olweus, Dan. *Bullying at School.* Cambridge, MA: Blackwell Publishers (1993).

Pipher, Mary. *Reviving Ophelia.* New York: Ballantine Books (1994).

Simmons, Rachel. *Odd Girl Out.* New York: Harcourt (2002).

Thompson, Michael. *Mom, They're Teasing Me.* New York: Ballantine Books (2002).

About the Authors

BRIDGET BARNES has been with Boys Town for 20 years, including five years as a Family-Teacher in our Long-Term Residential Program. She currently serves as program coordinator for Boys Town's Common Sense Parenting programs. As a parent trainer, Barnes has conducted hundreds of workshops for parents, caregivers, and professionals on topics related to children and families. She is the co-author of *Common Sense Parenting of Toddlers and Preschoolers.*

LAURA BUDDENBERG has been director of administration and outreach for the past five years at the Boys Town Center for Adolescent and Family Spirituality. She is a sought-after lecturer and trainer who has conducted workshops on topics ranging from media influence to cyberbullying. Buddenberg co-authored the books *Who's Raising Your Child? Battling the Marketers for Your Child's Heart and Soul* and *Unmasking Sexual Con Games.*

RAY BURKE, PH.D., has been with Boys Town since 1981, serving in a variety of direct care, training, and administrative positions, including as assistant director of Education Services and national director of parent training programs. He currently is the director of program evaluation for the National Resource and Training Center. Burke has provided consultation to a variety of child-care and educational organizations, and has authored numerous professional and self-help books (including *Common Sense Parenting*), manuals, and videotapes; grant applications; and articles for professional publications. He also has taught a variety of university courses and seminars related to parenting and family development.

JO C. DILLON is currently a site coordinator and Catholic schools coordinator with Boys Town's Education Training Department. A 13-year employee of Boys Town, she previously taught religion classes and helped pilot the Reading Is FAME® reading program at Boys Town's Wegner School. She is a co-author of *Tools for Teaching Social Skills in School.* During her more than 28 years as a teacher, Dillon taught in schools in Gretna and Omaha, Nebraska; Denver, Colorado; and Des Moines, Iowa.

MICHAEL HANDWERK, PH.D., is a child psychologist and the director of Clinical Services, Research, and Internship Training at Boys Town. He has been with the organization for nine years and has published more than 25 articles and chapters on the assessment and treatment of child and adolescent behavior problems. In addition to providing clinical services to youth in our programs, Handwerk counsels children and families from the Omaha area through the Boys Town Behavioral Pediatrics and Family Services Outpatient Clinic.

MICHELE HENSLEY has been with Boys Town for 10 years. Currently a program coordinator with the organization's Education Training Department, she has also served as an assistant site coordinator and as a science teacher at Father Flanagan High School. In 2005, she co-authored *Tools for Teaching Social Skills in School.* Prior to coming to Boys Town, Hensley taught science and math in Omaha, Nebraska, and taught science and physical education and coached volleyball, track, and cross country in San Antonio, Texas.

KATHLEEN MCGEE, M.A., is a religion educator, speaker, and author who has been with Boys Town for 15 years. In that time, McGee worked as a high school teacher where she helped create and pilot a relationship education curriculum for at-risk youth. She is the co-author of *Unmasking Sexual Con Games* and *Who's Raising Your Child? Battling the Marketers for Your Child's Heart and Soul.* McGee has presented workshops around the country on topics ranging from sexual harassment to child abuse. She currently serves as director of program services for the Boys Town Center for Adolescent and Family Spirituality.

DENISE PRATT has served as a trainer/consultant for teachers and administrators during her four years with Boys Town's Education Training Department. Pratt is also a co-author of *Tools for Teaching Social Skills in School.* She previously served as an experiential educator, teaching interpersonal skills to individuals from second-graders to adults. Her students included public-, private-, and home-schooled children, as well as adjudicated youth and youth in residential care with social and psychiatric diagnoses. She has also worked as a high school guidance counselor and assistant track coach.

About the Editors

JOSÉ BOLTON, SR., PH.D., L.P.C., is Associate Executive Director of the Boys Town National Resource and Training Center. In his position, he oversees a staff of more than 100 professionals working in diverse areas, from education training and behavioral health services to a national crisis hotline and publishing. Prior to joining Boys Town, Dr. Bolton had a highly successful 30-year career with the United States Air Force. He holds master's degrees from Mississippi State University, Troy State University, Chapman University, and Webster University. He has served as an administrator or faculty member at the United States Air Force Academy, Chapman University, the National Defense University, the Defense Equal Opportunity and Management Institute, and the Air Force Institute of Technology. He holds a doctorate in leadership and human behavior from United States International University.

STAN GRAEVE, M.A., has been with Boys Town for seven years. Currently an editorial supervisor, his previous positions included copywriter and marketing associate for the Boys Town Press and the National Resource and Training Center. Graeve has a master's degree in communication and a graduate certificate in human resources and training from the University of Nebraska at Omaha.

Index

Boys Town
Education Services

Boys Town's Education Services division provides other staff development training and assessments to teachers and administrators in elementary, middle, and secondary school settings. Our education experts share the concepts, strategies, and methods of the Boys Town Education Model through training such as:

THE WELL-MANAGED CLASSROOM
This training provides a deep understanding of the entire Education Model. Participants will learn how to foster an environment where students stay on task, accept responsibility and acquire the social skills necessary to be better self-managers.

SPECIALIZED CLASSROOM MANAGEMENT
This training teaches how to form relationships with students who have unique behavioral, emotional and social needs. Educators at alternative schools and special education settings have found this training extremely helpful. Learn to teach and interact with these students when they behave appropriately, inappropriately, or even when they are in crisis.

ADMINISTRATIVE INTERVENTION®
This training helps administrators reduce the frequency of office referrals by using intervention practices that support both the students and the teachers. You learn a consistent and effective step-by-step process to handle office referrals.

READING IS FAME®
Reading Is FAME is a research-based developmental reading program for adolescents who read below their grade level. The program is a series of four courses (Foundations, Adventures, Mastery, and Explorations) designed to appeal to adolescents.

Reading Is FAME is recognized by the National Staff Development Council (NSDC) and the National Education Association (NEA) as a content-specific program used to increase student achievement.

For more information about any of these programs visit our website, www.boystown.org or call us at 1-800-545-5771.

Boys Town, NE 68010 | www.boystown.org

Social Skill Lesson Plans for Teachers

Dealing with disruptive behaviors in the classroom can reduce the time a teacher has available for academic teaching. You can help prevent problem behaviors by teaching social skills to students. When children practice and learn how to behave in the classroom, they contribute to creating an environment that's calm, quiet, and conducive to successful learning.

Tools for Teaching Social Skills in School
ISBN: 1-889322-64-4

This book provides teachers with:

- Lesson plans for teaching 28 different social skills with activities that can be adapted for students in grades K-12. The plans include suggestions for discussion, activities, journaling, role-play, and reading.

- Reproducible skill pages that you can hand out or post in the classroom as reminders to students and coupons you can use to reward good behavior.

- Techniques and examples for "blending" the teaching of social skills into academic lessons in reading, writing, math, and social studies.

- Ideas for using bulletin board displays to motivate and monitor behavior.

- Strategies for increasing parent support.

The authors have a combined 40 years of teaching experience in K-12 classrooms and train teachers, administrators, and other school staff across the United States in the Boys Town Education Model. The Model emphasizes building relationships with students, teaching social skills, and reinforcement of positive behavior.

Available at bookstores or from the Boys Town Press.
1-800-282-6657 • www.boystownpress.org

Steps to 182 Social Skills and More!

Skill steps and useful teaching techniques

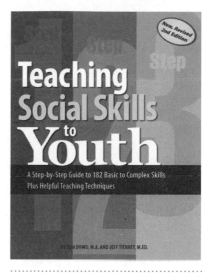

Teaching Social Skills to Youth features the step-by-step component behaviors to 182 skills, from the basic (following instructions and introducing yourself) to the complex (managing stress and resolving conflict). Opening chapters explain the individual and group teaching techniques that enable youth to recognize when, where, or with whom to use a particular skill. The authors also show how to plan skill-based treatment interventions for youth with difficult problems such as substance abuse, aggression, running away, depression, or attention deficits.

Teaching Social Skills to Youth, 2nd Edition
ISBN: 1-889322-69-5

New edition features helpful updates and CD-ROM

The second edition of this classic guide offers many updates and new features including:

- A CD-ROM that helps readers search for social skills by title, category, or problem behavior and allows you to print copies of social skill steps for display

- New information on how to help youth generalize the use of individual skills to varied social situations

- An index that cross-references the 182 skills to the Six Pillars of Character – respect, responsibility, trustworthiness, fairness, caring, and citizenship

- References to and information from the latest research findings

Teaching Social Skills to Youth is an ideal resource for the classroom, in counseling or therapy, and in job training programs. Use it to increase the skill competency of any child, help improve student behavior in school, or develop an individualized plan of treatment for troubled or at-risk youth.

Available at bookstores or from the Boys Town Press.
1-800-282-6657 • www.boystownpress.org

Credits

Book Cover and Layout: Anne Hughes
Front Cover Photography: Mike Buckley